Improbable Fiction

A comedy

Alan Ayckbourn

Samuel French — London
www.samuelfrench-london.co.uk

The right of Alan Ayckbourn to be identified as author of this work has been asserted by him in accordance with Section 77 of the Copyright, Designs and Patents Act 1988

Please see page iv for further copyright information

IMPROBABLE FICTION

First presented at the Stephen Joseph Theatre, Scarborough, on 26th May 2005, with the following cast:

Arnold	John Branwell
Ilsa	Laura Doddington
Brevis	Terence Booth
Vivvi	Claire Swinburne
Clem	Giles New
Jess	Becky Hindley
Grace	Eileen Battye

Directed by Alan Ayckbourn
Designed by Roger Glossop
Lighting by James Farncombe
Music by Denis King

CHARACTERS

Members of the Pendon Writers' Circle

Arnold Hassock, chairman, shop assistant (factual), late 40s
Jess Bales, farmer (historical romance), 40s
Grace Sims, housewife (children's fiction), 40s
Vivvi Dickins, journalist (crime fiction), 30s
Clem Pepp, council worker (science fiction), 30s
Brevis Winterton, retired schoolteacher (musical adaptations), 60s
Ilsa Wolby, shop assistant, about 18

The action takes place in the hall of Arnold's family home on the outskirts of a small country town.

Time — the present, more or less.

MUSIC

The music for the song *Light at the End of the Tunnel* by Denis King is available on hire from Samuel French Ltd.

> If this were played upon a stage now, I could condemn it as an improbable fiction.

Twelfth Night, Act III Scene 4

Other plays by Alan Ayckbourn published by Samuel French Ltd:

Absent Friends

Absurd Person Singular

Bedroom Farce

Body Language

Callisto 5

The Champion of Paribanou

A Chorus of Disapproval

Communicating Doors

Comic Potential

Confusions

A Cut in the Rates

Damsels in Distress:
FlatSpin, GamePlan
and RolePlay

Drowning on Dry Land

Ernie's Incredible Illucinations

Family Circles

Gizmo

Henceforward ...

House & Garden

How the Other Half Loves

Intimate Exchanges

It Could Be Any One of Us

Joking Apart

Just Between Ourselves

Man of the Moment

Mr A's Amazing Maze Plays

Mr Whatnot

My Very Own Story

The Norman Conquests:
Living Together,
Round and Round the Garden
and Table Manners

Relatively Speaking

The Revengers' Comedies

Season's Greetings

Sisterly Feelings

A Small Family Business

Snake in the Grass

Taking Steps

Ten Times Table

Things We Do for Love

This Is Where We Came In

Time and Time Again

Time of My Life

Tons of Money (revised version
of the farce by Will Evans and
Valentine)

Way Upstream

Wildest Dreams

Wolf at the Door (adapted from
Les Corbeaux by Henry Becque,
translated by David Walker)

Woman in Mind

A Word from Our Sponsor

ACT I

The hall/sitting room of Arnold's and his mother Elaine Hassock's home. The present, more or less. A week or so before Christmas, around 7 p.m.

It is a large twenties/thirties suburban, stockbroker mock-Tudor house on the outskirts of a small country town. Filled with sturdy furniture and uninteresting pictures, it was probably once very splendid, but is neglected of late. It has probably not altered much since the Hassocks first moved in nearly half a century ago

It is a large open hall with a staircase to a first floor short gallery above, which leads, in turn, to the bedrooms. At ground level, there is a front door opening directly on to the driveway with a set of hooks beside it, a doorway to the rest of the house (hereafter referred to as the "dining-room doorway") and another, more modest doorway, leading to the "below stairs" area, the kitchen, etc. Among the furnishings are a number of chairs, armchairs, that clearly belong in the room, plus a few extra upright chairs imported from the dining-room. These are arranged into a rough circle as if a meeting is soon expected. Seating is currently available for nine people. There is also a solid sideboard with a modern phone on it, occasional tables and, in one corner, a small grand piano. There is little or no sign that it is the festive season

At the start the Lights are on

After a moment, Arnold, a mild, ineffectual, pleasant-natured man in his late forties, enters from the upper gallery and starts to come downstairs

Arnold (*as he does so, calling to someone upstairs*) ... all right, Mother. I'm just popping downstairs ... She'll be here in a minute. I say, she'll be here in a minute ... (*Looking at his watch; to himself*) At least, I hope she'll be here in a minute, anyway. (*He stops in the centre of the circle of chairs and inspects the seating arrangement. To himself*) Now ... How many are we? (*Counting on his fingers*) Let's see, yours truly, Brevis, Jess ... four, five ... seven, eight, nine, ten ... Ten of us. And we've got ... let's see ... (*Starting to count the chairs in the circle, deliberately*)... One, two, three, four, five, six, seven, eight, nine, te— ... no, I've counted that one already ... (*Starting again*) ... One, two, three, four, five, six, seven, eight, ni— ... now, have I counted that one or haven't I? (*Starting yet again*) One, two ... come along get it together, Arnold ... one, two ...

The doorbell rings. A cheery ding-dong, not quite in keeping with the house

(*Hurrying to open the front door*) Oh, thank goodness ... (*As he opens it*) Come in! Come in! Come in, Ilsa!

He admits Ilsa, a girl of about eighteen from the local village, rosy-cheeked from the cold. She has on her winter coat and jeans beneath. She carries a motorbike helmet and a carrier bag

Ilsa (*a local accent*) 'evening, Arnold.
Arnold Good-evening, Ilsa. Come on in, you must be frozen.
Ilsa Bit cold, yes.
Arnold Kevin give you a lift, did he?
Ilsa Yes. He's going off to see his nan as usual. (*Calling back through the door, waving, mouthing*) 'Bye! See you later, Kev! Give her my love!

The sound of a motorbike roaring off

Arnold He's a good lad, isn't he, Kevin? Considerate.
Ilsa Kev likes his nan. He gets on with her fine. (*She starts to unbutton her coat*)
Arnold (*shutting the front door*) That's nice.
Ilsa Interesting, that.
Arnold What's that?
Ilsa How you can sometimes, you know, get on better with your grandparents than you do with your own parents. Interesting that. Like it skips a generation. I mean, I say things to my gran who's — I don't know — quite old really, about seventy, you know, that I'd never dream of saying to my mum. Not in a million years, I wouldn't. Interesting that.
Arnold Maybe your gran's got more time for you. Maybe your mum's a bit busy.
Ilsa You can say that again. Never stops, she doesn't. No, I usually get on better with older people, don't know why.
Arnold Except for Kevin of course.
Ilsa I don't count Kev. He's quite old, anyway. He's nearly thirty.
Arnold Well ...
Ilsa Cradle-snatcher, that's what my mum calls him. How's your mum this evening? Still the same, is she?
Arnold Still the same.
Ilsa No, well, you don't get better, do you, not from that. Once you've lost it, you've lost it for good. That's what they say, don't they?

Arnold Probably.

Ilsa My Uncle Ben, he had it. Wandered round the village with no clothes on.

Arnold Oh, dear.

Ilsa Thank your lucky stars she's bed-ridden ... At least your mum won't be doing that. (*Surveying the seating layout*) Got everything ready, have you? For your meeting? (*Moving to the kitchen door with her coat and belongings*) I'll just put these away. Then I'll give you a hand, Arnold.

Arnold (*indicating the hooks inside the front door*) You can leave those here, Ilsa.

Ilsa (*as she goes*) No, you'll need those, I'll leave these in the kitchen. You've got all those people coming. You'll need your hooks.

Ilsa goes off

Arnold There'll still be room for ... (*Giving up*) Oh, well. (*Returning to the chairs again*) One, two, three, four, five, six, seven, eight, nine ... ten. No, *not* ten. That's one again. (*Starting again*) Try it backwards ... nine, eight, seven — why can't I get this? — nine ... eight ... seven ...

Ilsa returns with her carrier bag

Ilsa You want any more chairs fetching, Arnold?

Arnold What? Oh. Six. No. Forgotten. What?

Ilsa Have you got enough chairs, have you?

Arnold I've no idea, I was just trying to count them, Ilsa. How many seats there, do you reckon?

Ilsa (*after a split-second pause*) Nine.

Arnold We need one more then.

Ilsa I'll get it.

Arnold We need ten. Probably.

Ilsa (*heading off*) Dining-room.

Ilsa goes off to the dining-room

The sound of thumping from the floor above

Arnold (*calling, up the stairs*) All right, Mother, just a minute! (*Regarding the chairs*) No, the trick, of course, is when you're counting not to stand in the middle. The trick is to stand on the outside and count.

Ilsa returns with another chair

Ilsa What's that?

Arnold I'm just saying, I should have stood on the outside.

Ilsa Right, probably. (*Placing her chair*) Ten. There you are. Want me to make your coffee at half-time, do you?

Arnold Now, you mustn't keep doing that, Ilsa. It's very kind of you but you're here to sit with Mother, not run after us.

Ilsa No trouble, doesn't take a sec. I'll just creep through, won't disturb you. She'll be asleep, time you want it. I'll read to her. That always sends her to sleep, the speed I read at.

Arnold I don't know where you find the patience. I've tried reading to her but it's hopeless. By the time I get to the end of the first paragraph, she's forgotten the title of the story.

Ilsa No, well. It's not really the story, is it? She just likes to know you're there. Perhaps I should read her one of yours?

Arnold No, Ilsa, I've told you, I don't write stories.

Ilsa You're a writer, though?

Arnold Of sorts, yes.

Ilsa So you could do. If you wanted to. Write stories.

Arnold No, no. My sort of writing, it's ... Well, I'm only part time, of course ... It's more — practical writing, you see. Instruction booklets and so on, you know. Actually, I'm doing quite a lot of instruction books these days. I think I may have nearly cornered the market.

Ilsa They're important, aren't they? Instruction books? We need booklets.

Arnold We do.

Ilsa Vital. Blow yourself up, otherwise.

Arnold Some of them are written ... well, I suppose it's English ... of sorts ... "strike manfully with palm of fist" ... I had to make sense of that the other day ... "jump up excitedly until fizzy", that was another one. I mean, people could have trouble interpreting those. Could lead to accidents.

Ilsa Especially if they're old folk.

Arnold Especially if they're any age.

Ilsa Anyway you're a writer. That's the point.

Arnold Well, I'm a renderer of English. Let's put it that way.

Ilsa You're too modest, Arnold. Better than me. I admire anyone who can write. Think of it. All of you, sitting here. All writers.

Arnold In our different ways.

Ilsa Do they get a lot of it — like — published in books, do they?

Arnold Well — not as much as some of them would like to. But the joy is in the writing, really, Ilsa. And some of them are really — very ... much more than I am.

Ilsa There you go again. You're the chairman, aren't you?

Arnold True. The chair, yes.

Ilsa Then stop running yourself down. You're the chairman.

Arnold The chair, yes. One or two of them prefer it if I call myself the chair.

Ilsa So you're the best then, if you're the chairman?

Arnold No, it really doesn't work like that, Ilsa. I'm the chair, mainly because — other people don't really fancy doing it — or don't have a lot of time — and, I suppose, I'm quite good at organizing guest speakers and — generally making lists ...

Ilsa And you've got this nice big house for you all to meet in.

Arnold Yes, I think that probably has a lot to do with it, too. A house that costs a fortune to heat. Ought to sell it really. Only, of course, she — Mother, wouldn't hear of it. When you've lived somewhere for nearly fifty years of your life, I suppose ...

Ilsa ... memories ...

Arnold Oh, she's plenty of those. My father, of course. She remembers him very clearly. I hear her talking to him some nights. She's quite clear and rational then. Like he's really there in the room with her. First time I heard her, I got out of bed to see if there wasn't someone there. Of course, there wasn't. Just in her mind, you know. But — it's like her whole life's unravelling, if you know what I mean. Her childhood, her marriage, her youth. Odd. Me, I can hardly remember last month.

Ilsa Last month! I can't remember last week. Nice for her, though, to be able to remember. Like an old photo album, isn't it?

Arnold Did your uncle remember at all?

Ilsa Uncle Ben? No, he didn't remember anything. He was just grumpy as hell. Kept taking off his clothes.

Arnold Oh, dear ...

Ilsa Relief to us all when he went, I can tell you. But with people like you ... anyway it's different, isn't it?

Arnold How do you mean?

Ilsa Well, you've got your imagination, haven't you? To fall back on? You can make up worlds of your own, can't you? You don't need to remember. You can just make them up for yourself, if you want to, can't you? See what I mean?

Arnold Yes, I take your point, Ilsa, but creative writing is largely based on memory, of course. I mean, when you say making it up — it's not totally original. It's more a — fusion — a reorganizing of past memories — our own — sometimes other people's, even ——

Ilsa You mean you steal them?

Arnold No, no, no. Well, occasionally we do. Shall we say inadvertently borrow them. But normally, you have an experience in your life and then — as — as an artist — you — re-interpret that experience. Into something other. Hopefully higher.

Ilsa (*impressed*) Brilliant. Is that what you do, then?

Arnold No, I keep saying, Ilsa, I just try to make sense of foreign instruction booklets, that's all. To be honest, the sad truth is that I've got as much creative imagination as that doorknob. And that's the truth.

Ilsa Rubbish.

Arnold Look, some people when they're woken up in the night by banging, they hear burglars — or they hear ghosts — or the central heating boiler about to explode. They hear all manner of things. Me? All I hear is banging. Pure and simple.

Ilsa Well, I think you're all right. You're very nice, as well.

Arnold Yes, well, that's kind of you to say so, Ilsa. Unfortunately, niceness has very little correlation to creativity, alas.

Ilsa Right.

The sound of more thumping on the floor above

Arnold (*calling up the stairs again*) Just a minute, Mother! Ilsa's just coming!

Ilsa I'd best get up there. (*Remembering her carrier*) Oh, look, I nearly forgot. You've got no Christmas decorations again, have you? You didn't last year either. Look, I bought you something, Arnold. Here. (*She produces a very small artificial Christmas tree in a plastic pot*) There! For you.

Arnold (*quite touched*) Oh, that's lovely, Ilsa. Thank you.

Ilsa (*fiddling with the base of the pot*) Look! Look! Wait! See? (*Switching it on*) Isn't that great? Look!

The tree is illuminated with tiny lights

Arnold Oh! Just look at that!

Ilsa (*handing him the tree*) Got it in Christmas Novelties.

Arnold You shouldn't have.

Ilsa Don't worry, I used my staff card. Got my discount.

Arnold Quite right, too. Well, thank you, Ilsa. I'm very, very touched.

Ilsa You deserve it. Ten days till Christmas, you need something. You were right. Useful, those staff cards, aren't they? Got all my presents from Cresswell's, this year. Practically. You get all yours there, did you?

Arnold No, well, I don't have — that many to get really. Another bedjacket for Mother but apart from that ... Not that she ever wears them. She just flings them off ... Now, I should have bought you something, Ilsa.

Ilsa Me? No ... I don't need presents. Not from you. Just glad to help, that's all.

Ilsa smiles at him. Arnold smiles back. A moment. It is interrupted by more thumping from above

Whoops! There she goes again!

Arnold Look, why don't you put this upstairs in Mother's room?

Ilsa In her room?

Arnold Be nice for her.

Ilsa It's for you.

Arnold Yes, I know. But that way we can both enjoy it.

Ilsa (*just a fraction disappointed*) Right. OK, then. (*She takes the tree back from him and starts up the stairs*)

Arnold (*aware he may have offended Ilsa slightly*) You ought to — you ought to sit in on our meeting one night, Ilsa.

Ilsa Me?

Arnold I'm sure we could find someone to be with Mother, just for ——

Ilsa You're joking. Me? Sitting with all those intellectuals?

Arnold Hardly.

Ilsa (*continuing up the stairs*) Wouldn't understand a word you're all talking about, would I?

Arnold I don't see why not. We're hardly ——

The doorbell chimes

Aha! Here they all come. Why don't you stay and ...

But Ilsa has hurried up the stairs and off

Arnold opens the front door

It is Jess, forties, with a healthy outdoor glow. She is dressed in casual farmer's gear with a worn sheepskin jacket. She has a briefcase

Good-evening, Jess. Glad you could make it. How are you?

Jess All right. How are you, Arnold?

Arnold Pretty fair, pretty fair.

Jess Your mum any better?

Arnold Much the same. We were just saying ——

Jess (*removing her coat; cheerfully*) Once they're there, they're there, aren't they? That's life, isn't it? I sometimes think the sooner it's all over the better. Bloody awful business, life, the whole thing. (*Of her coat*) Hang it up here, shall I? (*She hangs her coat on a hook*)

Arnold The farm not doing so well, then ...?

Jess Four ducks, thirteen chickens — correction *twelve* chickens, bloody fox got in again last night — a solitary cow, six new-born, unwanted kittens, and one old, nearly blind, seventeen-year-old incontinent collie doesn't constitute a farm, Arnold. By no stretch of the imagination. (*Holding out a paper bag*) Here. I brought you some eggs.

Arnold Oh, thank you so much. That is kind. Mother loves an egg.

Jess At least they're still laying, the ones that are left. Don't know for how
   much longer. Our chicken shed's like something out of an Agatha Christie
   novel. All eyeing each other, wondering who's going to be next.
Arnold Better suggest it to Vivvi. She could write it.
Jess Probably already has. Bitter out there. Going to be a storm later. Dog's
   jammed her arse under the Aga. Usually means a storm. Am I the first?
Arnold So far. Thank you for these. You really shouldn't.
Jess Well, I can't eat them all. And Po's allergic. So there you go. Either eat
   them or hurl them at the bloody town hall, either way.
Arnold And how is Polly?
Jess Po? She's fine. Usual bouncy self. Drives me up the wall some days but
   you have to love her.

The doorbell rings again

Arnold Excuse me.

*Jess moves away with her briefcase and sits in a chair and starts sifting pages
of notes, using the empty chair beside her as a desk*

Arnold opens the door again

   *It is Grace, also in her forties. In contrast to Jess, though, she is a pale,
   rather fraught, town-dweller. She is also dressed warmly and carries an
   artist's cardboard portfolio*

Grace Hallo.
Arnold Grace, come in, come in. You must be frozen.
Grace Bit nippy, isn't it? Am I the — (*seeing Jess*) Oh.
Jess Hallo.
Grace (*rather coolly*) Hallo, Jess.
Arnold (*helping Grace with her coat*) Come on the bus, did you, Grace?
Grace Yes, on the bus. On time for once, thank goodness.
Arnold Yes, you don't want to be standing around ...
Grace Not tonight.
Arnold Not tonight.
Grace (*admiring the room*) Oh, look. It's so lovely here, isn't it? It's lovely.
   I so love coming. Lovely and welcoming always, Arnold.
Arnold (*seeing Grace's portfolio*) Do I spy you've brought something with
   you tonight?
Grace Pardon? (*Shyly*) Oh, well. Maybe. I don't know.
Arnold Something you're going to share with us, Grace?
Grace (*with a slight glance towards Jess*) Well, we'll see.

Arnold Hear that, Jess? Grace has brought something to share with us.

Jess (*unimpressed, without looking up*) Good-o.

Arnold Well, I'm excited. Not before time, Grace.

Grace Well, we'll see.

Arnold How's the family?

Grace Oh, you know. Wanetta's doing well. Just sitting her A levels. And Delwyn, he — well, we don't hear from him very much since he went off to London.

Arnold What's he doing there, exactly?

Grace We don't exactly know. We don't even know where he is, exactly. Actually. Except he's in London. Somewhere.

Arnold Oh, dear, that must be worrying.

Grace Yes, it is a bit. For me anyway. I don't think Jeff cares one way or the other. Good riddance. That's all he says.

Arnold Well, he's probably joking, you never know.

Grace No, not Jeff. Jeff never jokes. Not these days.

Arnold (*waving the paper bag he still holds*) Yes, I'm just going to pop these in the fridge. Keep them fresh. Eggs. From Jess.

Grace Right.

Arnold hurries out to the kitchen. Grace is left alone with Jess

(*Awkwardly*) Well.

Jess (*still absorbed*) Still stuck with that bloody awful man, then?

Grace Yes. (*Slight pause*) Still stuck with that bloody awful woman?

Jess At least she doesn't beat me.

Grace Neither does Jeff.

Jess (*disbelieving*) Hmm. Hmm. Hmm. Hmm.

Grace (*after a slight pause*) You wouldn't understand, anyway.

Jess What precisely wouldn't I understand?

Grace You wouldn't understand the pressure they're under sometimes. Men? You wouldn't understand that, would you?

Jess I understand enough not to share my life with the buggers. I've more sense than that.

Grace What could you possibly know? Possibly? (*She sits in a chair at a distance from Jess — there are four chairs between them*)

The doorbell goes

Pause

Jess (*without looking up*) Doorbell.

Grace (*without moving*) So it is.

Arnold returns from the kitchen

Arnold Was that the doorbell?
Grace Oh, yes. I think it probably ... (*She half-heartedly makes to rise*)
Arnold Let them in, then. Too cold to stand out there.

The doorbell rings again

(*Calling*) Just coming!

Arnold opens the front door

> *Vivvi, in her thirties, effusive and attractive, waits with Clem, mid-thirties,
> a silent, rather awkward man who some, perhaps uncharitably, might
> describe as a nerd. They would not be too wide of the mark. Clem has a
> briefcase; Vivvi, a large shoulder bag*

Vivvi (*singing*) "The first Noël ..." (*Excitedly*) Let us in! Let us in!
Arnold (*cheerfully*) Yes, come in, Vivvi, come in.
Vivvi (*moving into the room*) Brrrrrrrr!
Arnold 'Evening, Clem.
Clem 'Evening. (*He follows Vivvi inside*)

Arnold closes the door

Arnold (*to Clem*) Vivvi give you a lift, did she?
Clem Yes. (*He takes off his coat, hangs it up and then goes and sits down
by himself, next to Grace and anticlockwise from her*)
Vivvi (*also removing her coat and hanging it up*) Hallo, you two. (*She sits,
two seats away, anticlockwise, from Clem*)

Arnold sits two seats away, clockwise, from Grace

Grace Hallo.
Jess Hi.
Vivvi Happy Christmas — nearly. Now, I have masses of apologies, I'm
afraid.
Arnold Oh, dear.
Vivvi From Bernard who's skiing with the family, of course. And Gerald,
who's going down with something and doesn't know what. And abject
apologies from Sally who has relatives. And Paula who's already gone to
Scotland for Christmas and New Year.

Arnold I know, it's a bad time to have a meeting, I said it was, last time. How about Ray?

Vivvi Don't know. Haven't heard from Ray at all. Not for weeks.

Jess I think he's abroad, as well.

Vivvi Is he?

Jess I have a feeling he said something last time. What about Brevis? Is he coming?

Vivvi God knows.

Grace I certainly hope not.

Vivvi laughs. It's a nervous laugh at the slightest hint of tension

Arnold (*to Jess; playfully*) Now, now, now. Well, I don't know, what's the time? It's only just gone half past. (*Looking at them all in turn*) Should we give Brevis a minute longer?

Vivvi Yes. Better give him a minute.

Jess shrugs

Clem Don't mind either way.

Grace Listen, if Mr Winterton — Brevis — is coming then I certainly shan't be showing my work, I'd like that minuted, please.

Arnold Oh, dear, we won't have anyone to take the minutes, will we? Not if Paula's away.

Vivvi I'll do it.

Arnold Oh, would you mind, Vivvi? Thank you very much.

Vivvi No problem. I have shorthand. Let me through, I'm a journalist! (*She produces a notebook and pencil during the following*)

Jess More than Paula has.

Arnold No, I won't hear a word against Paula, Jess ...

Grace Hear! Hear!

Jess I've nothing against Paula personally. I just wish to God her minutes bore some resemblance to our actual meetings. I appreciate this is a Creative Writing Group, but I don't think that necessarily includes the minutes.

Vivvi laughs

Grace Oh no, that's unfair. Just because Paula isn't here to defend herself — If some of us in this group had done half as much as Paula's done ...

Arnold Yes, all right, all right, Grace.

Grace Paula has worked her fingers to the bone, Jess ...

Arnold Yes, all right, Grace, point taken.

Grace Well. Honestly.

Arnold Perhaps we could minute it, Vivvi, that the meeting passed a vote
of thanks to Paula, Mrs Boon, in absentia, for all the hard work she has put
in during the past year.

Vivvi (*who now has her notebook and pencil poised*) Right.

Arnold All agreed? Grace? Vivvi?

Vivvi (*writing*) Sure.

Arnold Clem?

Clem Either way.

Arnold Jess?

Jess (*shrugging, reluctantly*) If you like.

Arnold Thank you, Jess. (*Looking at his watch*) Well, I do think now we
ought to be making a start, Brevis or no Brevis. It's thirty-four minutes past
so ——

Vivvi Did you say you'd brought something to show us, Grace?

Grace Yes, but if Mr Winterton is going to be here, I don't intend to —
I mean, he'd just ... You see I still call him that. He hasn't taught me for
twenty years and he still terrifies me. He used to make us stand out in
the ——

Vivvi Well, he's not here yet, is he? Come on, let's have a quick look, a sneak
preview, can we?

Arnold Why not? We've all waited long enough, Grace. The suspense has
been killing us. I think we deserve a look, don't you?

Grace (*clasping her portfolio*) Well. All right. I think, before I show you, you
ought to know the circumstances of how I came to write this. Write it ...

Jess (*muttering*) Oh, for God's sake ...

Grace (*with a glare at Jess*) ... to create this ... I started this several years ago
when both my children were still very tiny. I intended to write them
something that would be both edifying and amusing and instructive. That
they could take with them as they grew up. If you see what I mean.

Arnold Excellent. Yes. Splendid.

Grace There's so little these days — or even in those days — that's really
edifying. I think. Especially for young children. It's all terrible TV trash,
isn't it?

Arnold Yes. I don't see a lot of television. Mother has a set in the bedroom.
I catch a glimpse of it occasionally. It's really quite alarming some of it.

Grace Well, I meant more the written stuff, really. It's all very — whatever
the opposite of uplifting is, I suppose.

Jess (*drily*) Downlifting.

Vivvi laughs

Grace So the point is, I tried to write something for them myself, my
children, to try to fill the vacuum. Try to fill it.

Arnold And how did they like it? Did they appreciate it?

Grace No, the point is, I started it — but I never got to finish it, you see. Finish it. Other — things — family things — got in the way. So they never got to see it. And Jeff said I was wasting my time anyway so I — I sort of gave up.

Vivvi So they never saw it at all?

Grace No.

Vivvi Oh, how sad. I didn't realize.

Grace But, then I thought, why not have another go? So I dug it out of the attic. And I'm seriously trying to finish it this time. You know, finish it.

Vivvi Good for you.

Arnold Never too late, no. How old are they now, the children?

Grace Wanetta is sixteen and Delwyn's eighteen.

Vivvi And what's your book called? Does it have a name?

Grace "The Exciting Adventures of Doblin the Goblin."

Vivvi Ah.

Arnold Well, they may be a trifle old. But there'll be others. Younger children. Coming up.

Grace (*a trifle alarmed*) Not from me. No, no, never ...

Arnold No, no. I meant generally. Children. Everywhere. Aren't there? Lots of them, all in need of a good read.

Vivvi May we look, Grace? Will you let us have a look?

Grace All right. (*She unfastens the portfolio*) A lot of it is pictures, of course. Because, as you probably know, I was trained originally as an artist, of course ... I have these pictures ... (*She produces a sheaf of brightly-coloured illustrations*) Perhaps you'd like to — pass them round, Arnold. They're in order but ... well, you'll see ...

During the following, Grace passes the pictures round clockwise to Arnold over the empty chair between them; Arnold, in turn, passes them to Jess over the two empty chairs between them; Jess, in turn, passes the pictures to Vivvi over the empty chair between them; Vivvi then passes them to Clem over the empty chair between them; Clem finally passes them directly back to Grace. Jess gives the pictures barely a glance. Clem feigns some interest but isn't very convincing. It is left to Arnold and Vivvi to make up for their unenthusiastic colleagues

Arnold Oh! Oh! These are splendid. Splendid, Grace! I knew you were an artist but, no ... I had no idea.

Grace That's at the start of the book. At the start, when Doblin first emerges out of his winter burrow ...

Arnold Yes, I can see, I can see. You can just see his little head popping out of the hole there, can't you ... (*Passing on the picture*) Here, Jess, take a look at that. Isn't that splendid?

Jess (*cursorily*) Oh, yes. (*She passes the picture on to Vivvi*)

Arnold Isn't that wonderful, Vivvi? What do you think?

Vivvi Oh, it's brilliant, Grace. Brilliant. What a waste.

Grace How do you mean?

Vivvi Well, that you haven't, you know, taken them any ... further ... (*Passing the picture to Clem*) Look, Clem.

Arnold She's intending to, Vivvi. That's the point. Grace is planning to ...

Clem (*looking at the picture*) Fantastic.

Arnold Clem likes them. Look, Clem likes them.

Clem Great. (*He passes the picture back to Grace*)

Arnold Come on, Grace. Any more, are there? Pass them round.

Grace (*taking up a second picture*) This is a bit later on, when Doblin's out of his burrow. He's standing in the big meadow, looking round, you see? (*She passes the picture to Arnold*)

Arnold Oh, yes, there he is again ...

Grace Looking round. You can see how small he is beside the buttercup. You can tell from the size of the buttercup, you see.

Arnold Oh yes, huge. It's a huge buttercup. Cheery little chap, isn't he? Seems to be always smiling.

Grace This is early on, of course. Early in the book. Before things go wrong for Doblin.

Arnold (*passing the picture to Jess*) Oh, dear, do they?

Vivvi Not too wrong, I hope?

Grace No. Not too ... You know. Just — adversity.

Jess Wipe the grin off his face. (*She passes the picture on to Vivvi*)

Vivvi laughs

Arnold It's only intended for little children though, isn't it? You don't want to frighten them, do you?

Grace No, but even at that age they still have to learn, don't they?

Vivvi I think they're lovely, Grace. And they all illustrate this story you've written, do they?

Grace They will eventually, yes ...

Arnold Have you got the story? Could you read us a little?

Grace Well, I'm — that's the bit where I got a bit stuck. I mean, it's all here in my head, you know, but I haven't really written — managed to write it down properly. Not yet. Not properly. (*Taking up a third picture*) Look, you see, here's Doblin climbing the tree, trying to find out where he is. (*She passes the third picture to Arnold*)

Vivvi Doesn't he know?

Grace No, you see. In my story, when goblins fall asleep, when they hibernate, they forget everything they knew. When they wake up, they can remember nothing at all.

Arnold Bit like my mother. Anyway, he's still smiling, isn't he? (*He passes the third picture to Jess*)

Jess (*barely giving the picture a glance before passing it on to Vivvi*) So when are you intending to write the book?

Grace As I say, I ——

Jess I mean, I only ask because this is a writers' group, you know. I just wondered when you were going to get down to the actual business of writing ——

Arnold Very soon, Jess, you heard Grace. Very soon.

Jess Only otherwise, perhaps you ought to think about joining an artists' group.

Vivvi (*laughing*) Look at this, Clem. Isn't it lovely?

Clem Lovely.

Arnold You're having problems setting out the story you say, Grace?

Grace Yes. It's how I write it. I really want it to be in verse.

Arnold Verse, I see.

Jess Rhyming couplets, no doubt?

Grace Possibly.

Arnold Nothing wrong with a good rhyming couplet.

Jess Dear God! When did you last hear a good rhyming couplet.

Vivvi Rupert Bear books are full of them. (*She laughs*)

Clem I like Rupert. My mother still gives me the annuals. Every Christmas.

Jess Now, why am I not surprised by that?

Grace (*taking up a fourth picture*) And here he is again. He's decided to sail off down the stream. You see, there he is, sailing off in a walnut shell that he's borrowed. (*She passes it to Arnold*)

Arnold Oh, yes. Who's he borrowed it from, then?

Jess From a walnut, presumably.

Vivvi laughs

Grace No, from a squirrel. Sid Squirrel. See? You can just make out his nose.

Arnold Oh, yes. I see him, the rascal. He's smiling too, isn't he?

Jess Bloody vermin. Shoot them on sight, I do.

Arnold Oh, no. He's a friendly squirrel, Jess. You wouldn't want to shoot him. Have a look —— (*He makes to pass the next picture over to Jess*)

Jess Yes, great. Look — how many more of these, are there? I don't want to be a killjoy but I do think we ought to get on with the meeting, don't you?

Arnold Yes, Jess, point taken. But I do think we owe Grace here her moment of glory. We've all had our moments over the past months. And Grace has sat through them all very patiently, never complaining ...

Jess No, fair enough. All I'm saying is ——

The doorbell chimes

Arnold Whoops! A latecomer. You never know, it might be Brevis.
Grace (*alarmed*) Oh.

*Arnold goes to the door, leaving one of Grace's pictures on the chair to
his* L

*Grace puts away the pictures, back into her portfolio. She fails to see the one
on the chair to Arnold's* L

Vivvi I wonder what's made him so late?
Clem Maybe the chain came off his bike again. (*He smirks*)

Arnold opens the door

> *Brevis is there in his cycling mac. He still has on his cycle clips. He is sixty-
> five, irascible and generally tetchy. It's probably his age*

Arnold Oh yes, it is, it's Brevis. Come in, Brevis.
Brevis Bastards! Bastards!
Arnold Sorry?
Brevis (*to anyone and everyone in general*) You know, I taught kids for over
forty years. Forty years. And I never begrudged a moment of it. I did it
willingly, I undertook it freely, happily, the ups the downs, the highs the
lows. I gave my life to teaching. To kids. And I am now sixty-five years
of age and, do you know, I've just realized that I hate the little bastards. I
loathe them with every fibre of my being. I resent every second of the life
I wasted on them. I have wasted my life, do you hear? You are looking at
a man with a totally wasted life.

Vivvi laughs. Brevis gives her a look

Arnold What happened, Brevis?
Brevis (*calmer*) They let my tyres down. I left the bike outside the flat for
half a minute and the little bastards let my tyres down. That's why I'm late.
Arnold It might not have been children. (*He sits*)
Brevis (*taking off his mac and hanging it up*) Of course it was kids, who else
could it be? I hate them. Wipe them all out, I say.
Clem Then we'd run out of adults.
Brevis Oh, hallo, Einstein, you're here, are you? Met any good aliens lately?
Clem Not until you came in. (*He smirks*)
Brevis Sorry I'm late, anyway. Blame the vandals. (*He is about to sit down
next to Arnold when he sees Grace's picture on the chair*) What the hell's
this?
Grace (*reaching to take it, hastily*) Oh, sorry. I meant to ... I meant to ...

Brevis What's it supposed to be?

Arnold It's an illustration from Grace's new book, Brevis.

Brevis What book?

Grace A children's book, that's all. It ——

Brevis Oh, I see. Your children did this, did they, Sims?

Grace No, I did. I did that.

Vivvi (*laughing*) Grace did that.

Brevis You did this?

Grace Yes.

Brevis I see. (*He stares at it*) Well, maths never was the strongest subject in your family, was it? Neither you nor your wretched son.

Vivvi That's artwork, Brevis. Nothing to do with maths.

Brevis If you'd paid more attention to your basic geometry, Grace, you might have learnt a bit more about drawing perspective. Look at this bloke here, he's completely out of scale with this huge flower. He's tiny.

Grace I know he's tiny, he's ——

Brevis What's he meant to be sitting in here? It looks like a nut.

Grace It is a nut.

Brevis Is it? What the hell's he doing sitting in a nut?

Grace He's a goblin.

Brevis He's a what?

Grace A goblin.

Brevis (*to the others*) I actually taught her, you know. (*Shaking his head*) A wasted life! A wasted life! (*He hands the picture back to Grace like a teacher returning homework*)

Grace (*taking the picture, softly*) Thank you.

Grace, crushed, puts away the picture with the others and refastens her portfolio

Arnold Well, Grace, many congratulations, well done. I hope you'll be keeping us *au fait* with your progress over the months to come. Now, I really do think, since Brevis is here, that it's time to start our meeting proper.

Jess About time.

Arnold Now, I feel that in view of the low turnout this evening due to seasonal and other unavoidable matters we might make this a fairly brief meeting — if everyone's agreeable — and perhaps just restrict it to maybe a reflection — a look back, if you like — on our exciting meeting of last month — and the lessons to be drawn from that. And then perhaps we can wind up with our usual brief individual reports of current work in progress. And I must, as always, emphasize the word brief.

Brevis Please.

Vivvi (*smiling*) All right, all right!

Arnold Now, I wasn't just meaning you, Vivvi. We can all be a bit guilty occasionally. Now, first of all, last month. You will recall, of course — and I think everyone present was there — the visit we had from the distinguished novelist H.F.Cataxian — or as he asked us to refer to him, Harry. Now, I'd welcome your reactions to Harry's stimulating talk ——

Grace Huh!

Arnold — whatever they may be. I think we can agree it was certainly stimulating. But what conclusions can we draw for ourselves, do you think?

Grace Well ——

Arnold Grace, sorry, just a moment, if I may, just let me finish — sorry. What conclusions for us personally? Well, I think his overriding theme — and I don't want in any way to over-simplify what Harry was saying — not at all — but the over-riding message that I got from him was this. If you feel you're a writer, if you deep-down believe you're a writer, then for God's sake get on with the writing. I think when he finally finished — and we surely must agree, whatever else, we certainly got our money's worth — when Harry finally finished the over-riding feeling we all had — and I do exclude you, Vivvi, in this — the feeling was that we were all holding back in some way. Failing to practise a craft we all believed, in our different ways, we had a destiny to pursue. If you recall, Harry ended his talk by throwing down a challenge to us all — (*producing a scrap of paper*) — and I wrote it down. (*Reading*) "If you believe you can write — and why the hell else are you all here otherwise? — then" — and I'm quoting his own words here — "then get the — eff word — on with it."

Vivvi laughs

Brevis I don't think you've quite finished — he ended up, surely, "you bunch of wankers".

Arnold Well, I didn't think that was — in the present circumstances — quite appropriate to quote.

Ilsa appears at the top of the stairs

Jess It was totally appropriate. He was probably right. We are all wankers ...

They all see Ilsa. Vivvi laughs

Arnold Ah. Ilsa. Going to make our coffee now, are you? Thank you.

Ilsa smiles shyly at them and tiptoes down the stairs

We could all do with some coffee, I think, Ilsa. By the way, there are some mince pies out there as well, I meant to tell you. If you want to pop them in the microwave ...

Ilsa nods and goes out to the kitchen

(*To the others*) Not home-made, I'm afraid. Cresswell's finest. Mother's hardly up to that these days. That's Ilsa. You've all met Ilsa Wolby, haven't you? She works with me at Cresswell's, of course. Yes.

Vivvi Yes, she's been before, hasn't she? Attractive.

Arnold Oh, yes.

Vivvi When she smiles.

Arnold Yes. Anyway. Reactions to Mr Cataxian. Anybody?

Vivvi Well ...

Grace I thought he was really very offensive. I mean, we all paid good money — quite a lot of money in fact to have a talk — which I'd hoped would be informative and helpful and constructive and then all the man does is stand there telling pointless anecdotes and using obscenities.

Clem He was drunk.

Arnold Oh, come now ...

Grace He was certainly drunk ...

Vivvi ... and he got more drunk as the evening went on.

Arnold I don't see how he could have done that ——

Grace He had a flask.

Arnold Did he?

Vivvi We all saw the flask. Surely you saw the flask, Arnold?

Arnold No, I can't say I did. I was probably paying too much attention to what he was saying. I was trying to make notes, you see, at the same time.

Brevis Who the hell was he, anyway? I'd never heard of him.

Arnold He was — H.F. Cataxian. I'm sure he ——

Brevis I went to the library. Nothing of his in there. Not a single book.

Vivvi Nor the bookshop in town. They'd never heard of him.

Brevis They've never heard of anybody that place. I went in there the other day, you won't believe this, to order a new copy of *The Pilgrim's Progress* — my old copy was getting a bit dog-eared — and the girl said, "Oh, I don't think they've made a book out of that." And I said, "What on earth are you talking about, it is a book, girl. It's reputedly the first piece of fiction ever to be written in the English language." "Oh really?" she said, "I thought you meant the movie, *Private's Progress.*"

Arnold Oh, dear.

Brevis And I said, "No, *The Pilgrim's Progress.* John Bunyan, woman. Have you never heard of John Bunyan?" And she said, "Oh yes, sorry, I'm with you now. *The Thirty-Nine Steps* and all that." Dear God. To think I probably taught that girl at some stage.

Arnold Ah, but you'd have taught her mathematics, Brevis.
Brevis I'd have taught her nothing.
Clem What's *The Thirty-Nine Steps*, then?
Vivvi It's a thriller. You ought to read it.
Clem I only read sci-fi.
Arnold Anyway. Getting back to our guest, Mr Cataxian ——
Clem I looked him up ...
Grace You did?
Clem On the internet. He has his own site on the internet.
Brevis What does that prove? Everybody's got their own site on the internet.

Vivvi laughs

Clem No, they don't, that's nonsense ——
Brevis Jess's dog's probably got his own site on the internet. Being on the
internet proves absolutely nothing. I tell you, the internet is the biggest
repository for junk, rubbish and useless information ever known to the
human race. Every lunatic opinion, every crackpot theory ...
Clem It's an opportunity for ordinary people to express what they feel ——
Brevis (*warming to his subject; excitedly*) Exactly. Ordinary people. I'm
sick to death of ordinary people, you know that? What do you think makes
them ordinary, Clem? They're ordinary because they don't have any
original opinions of their own. They don't have a single interesting thing
of any importance to say. And now we've got that bloody internet thing,
they're all saying it. What's worse, they're all talking to each other.
Exchanging their batty views. They're proliferating, breeding ever fresh
lunacies. And, as a result, the whole world, the whole of civilization is
spiralling down, down, down, towards the lowest common denominator,
till we have people like you who have never even heard of John Buchan.

Clem sits battered by the onslaught. Brevis, mercifully, pauses for breath

Arnold Anyway, getting back to Mr Cataxian, quite apart from his —
colourful language — was there anything we could learn from him?
Lessons we could take away?
Vivvi That good manners don't cost anything. (*She laughs*)

Brevis shrugs. Clem says nothing

Arnold Well, I'm sorry if you all feel it was a waste of your time. And, of
course more important, money. As I said, I did try originally to get P.D.
James but she was otherwise committed, so when the agent ... Still. We
weren't to know, were we?

Jess I think I learnt something from him.

Arnold Jess, really? Did you?

Jess Yes. He did have a — colourful turn of phrase — nothing I haven't used myself, mind you — but what he said made good sense. Be honest, we do tend to spend a lot of our time simply talking about writing, don't we? Rather than getting down and actually doing it. He was quite right. I do, certainly, as you know full well. I get nervous. Terrified. But it's like taking exercise. Ideally, we ought to do it every day. Hark at me.

Grace There's a danger you can over-write.

Jess Possibly. Hardly applies to either of us though, does it? Anyway, Grace, he certainly got you going again, didn't he? Don't knock the man.

Grace I can assure you that nothing he — absolutely nothing he said ——

Jess Look, I'm not saying we should publish everything — we should be so lucky — but the secret is to keep writing. That's all he was saying. Or alternatively give it up completely and go and play golf. If you're not enjoying it, which I'm certainly not at present, then it's torment. I mean, come on, it's got to be fun, at least, hasn't it? Rewarding? Otherwise what are we all doing it for? Not for the money, that's for sure. What else are we doing it for but our own pleasure? (*She pauses, rather startled by her own outburst*)

Vivvi laughs

Jess Sorry.

Arnold Well said, Jess. I hope you were paying attention to yourself then. Very good advice.

Jess Well ...

Arnold Look, how about this for an idea? Just off the top of my head, this one. What if we all concentrated on one particular topic. Like, I don't know, golf. No, not golf. Something we all know about. There must be something. And then we all agree to write about it from our various angles. Just as an exercise.

Vivvi But we all of us write such different things ...

Arnold Yes, I know. But maybe we could all come together. Just for the sake of the exercise ——

Vivvi ... different styles. I mean, I write thrillers. And Jess writes romances ——

Jess Historical romances. Rather I'd like to write historical romances.

Vivvi And Clem writes — well, Clem writes his science fiction ...

Clem Science fact.

Vivvi And Grace is — she's working on her children's book, isn't she ——

Arnold And I write instruction manuals, I take your point, Vivvi. You couldn't find a more different bunch, that's what I'm saying. We've all got a bit stuck in our separate own ruts, haven't we? Now, wouldn't it be good to combine, for once? I mean, let's face it, it's a very lonely business writing, sometimes.

Jess Not a bad idea.

Grace How could we ever agree on anything we all of us wanted to write about? Impossible.

Brevis What about me? Where do I fit in? I write musicals, don't I?

Arnold Well, you could — write a piece of music on the subject — put some songs in — anyway, you do more than music, Brevis, don't be so modest. You do the words as well.

Brevis I do the book. I don't do lyrics, though, I never do lyrics.

Arnold I'm sure we could find a way to incorporate you. You know, I think this is rather exciting. Well worth thinking about, the more I think of it. If we could ——

From upstairs there comes sudden thumping on the floor above. They all look up

Oh, dear. Mother's feeling abandoned. Ilsa's left her on her own while she makes the coffee. (*Rising*) I'd better ... Excuse me. Look, think about that idea. I really think it's worth a thought. Won't be a minute.

Arnold goes off upstairs

There is a slight pause

Vivvi It would never work. Would it?

Jess It might.

Vivvi I mean, it would have to be something so neutral ... Something we all of us know about. (*She thinks*) Shopping?

Brevis Dear God!

Vivvi Well, we all do that. We all go shopping, don't we? (*She laughs*)

A slight pause

Clem We could imagine what intelligent life will be like in a hundred years.

Brevis There won't be any.

Vivvi laughs. A slight pause

Jess What about a love story. The first time we all fell in love. We've all done that, surely? Loved ones? Pets? Wives? Husbands? Children?

Grace gives an involuntary sniff

Sorry.

A slight pause

Vivvi There must be something.

At this point, Ilsa enters with the coffee tray. On it are six cups, coffee pot, milk, sugar, six side plates and a dish of pre-heated, shop-made mince pies. Ilsa is concentrating hard on keeping the load balanced

Ah!
Jess (*without moving*) Can you manage, dear?

Ilsa moves to the sideboard. They all sit watching her

Grace (*as they watch; whispering*) Big tray for her ...
Vivvi (*whispering*) Yes ...
Grace (*whispering*) Must be heavy ...
Vivvi (*whispering*) Yes ...

There is no conversation whilst Ilsa pours the coffee, initially black, into the cups. She takes round a pair of cups in turn, starting with Brevis and Jess, then clockwise round the circle to Vivvi and Clem and finally to Grace. The others watch her. Or rather they watch her when they think that Ilsa cannot see them watching her. Ilsa, embarrassed, is all too aware of their stares and of their lack of conversation. During this:

Brevis (*taking his cup*) Thank you.
Jess (*likewise*) Thank you, dear.
Vivvi (*likewise*) Thank you so much.
Clem (*likewise*) Thanks.
Grace (*likewise*) Thank you.

Ilsa returns to the sideboard

(*Whispering to Vivvi*) Does she speak English at all?
Vivvi (*whispering*) No idea. I've never heard her speak.

Ilsa now takes round the milk jug and sugar, starting with Brevis

Brevis (*declining both*) No, thank you.
Jess Thank you. Just a drop. (*She pours milk into her cup. Declining sugar*) No, thank you.
Vivvi Thank you. (*She pours milk into her cup. Declining sugar*) No, thanks.

Clem Thanks. (*He pours the milk into his cup. Accepting sugar*) Yes.
Grace Just a weeny bit. (*She puts a splash of milk in her coffee. Declining sugar*) No, thank you.

Ilsa returns to the sideboard once more

(*Whispering to Vivvi*) I think she's probably foreign.

Vivvi nods

Ilsa starts again, this time bringing round the side plates and the plate of six mince pies. The others start to speak to Ilsa more deliberately now

Brevis No, thank you.
Vivvi Not having a mince pie, Brevis?
Brevis Can't stand them. Up all night.
Jess (*taking a plate and accepting one*) Thank you, dear.
Vivvi (*taking a plate and accepting one*) Yum! Yum! Yes, please! Yes!
Clem (*taking a plate and taking two pies*) Thanks. I'll have his.
Grace No, thank you.
Vivvi No, Grace?
Grace (*patting her stomach*) Trying not to.

Ilsa passes back by Clem

Clem I'll have hers as well, then. (*He takes a third mince pie*)
Jess Clem!
Clem What's wrong?

Arnold enters and comes downstairs

Ilsa moves back to the sideboard and pours Arnold's coffee

Arnold Oh, Ilsa, well done. Thank you very much. Did you bring the mince — ? (*Seeing she has*) — Yes, you did. (*Noticing Clem's plate*) Hope you saved one for me.
Jess Just.
Arnold Hold on, Ilsa, let me.

Arnold and Ilsa stand together at the sideboard. The others watch them. Ilsa gives Arnold his coffee. An innocent, intimate ritual

Thank you.

She pours him his milk

Thank you.

She hands him a plate

Thank you.

She offers him a mince pie

(*Accepting*) Thank you.

Arnold stays by the sideboard. Ilsa walks self-consciously back up the stairs

(*As Ilsa reaches the top*) Thank you very much, Ilsa.

Ilsa turns and gives Arnold a bright, brief smile and goes

A silence, of which Arnold seems quite unaware

Nice girl, Ilsa. Really nice. I've grown very fond of her, I really have. There you are, Brevis. You talk to her, she'll restore your faith in modern youth. Yes, she's really pleasant.

A slight pause. Vivvi laughs

Right. Where were we? What are we all going to write about, then? Anyone had any bright ideas?

They all fail to meet his gaze

Oh. Never mind. Let's make a vow then, shall we, to come along with an idea in time for the next meeting. Let's make it our New Year resolution. Yes? Good. Moving along then. Work in progress. Grace? I think we've already heard from you. An exciting project and we all wish you luck with it.

Grace Thank you.

Arnold And you will promise to bring something along to show us next time, won't you?

Grace I'll try. If I can — I mean, I'll try. If I can ...

Arnold That's a promise. So who's next for the hot seat? Clem? Any fresh developments with the book? What's it called again, *The Conspiracy ...?*

Clem *The Conspirators.*

Arnold Oh, beg your pardon. Any more updates, Clem? Bit of a cliff-hanger, this one, isn't it?

Clem produces some fresh typed sheets from his briefcase

Clem Yes, I know last time some of you had trouble following it for some
reason. I don't know why because it's perfectly clear if you listen but this
time I've taken the precaution of printing out some copies of the synopsis
— of the story so far.
Arnold What a good idea.
Clem I've made copies. I'll pass them round, shall I?
Arnold Of course.

*Clem hands Grace a pile of typed synopses, probably about four sheets of A4
stapled together*

   (*To Grace*) Would you mind?
Grace No, of course ... (*She takes one and hands them to Arnold*)
Arnold Right, yes. This is detailed, Clem. (*Keeping one*) Brevis ...

*Brevis takes the pile and immediately passes it on to Jess without taking a
copy*

   Don't you need a copy?
Brevis After last time, it's engraved on my memory.

*Vivvi laughs. Jess keeps one and passes it to Vivvi. Vivvi passes the rest of the
pile back to Clem*

Clem Right. Everyone got one who wants one? Right. I'm going to read from
the start of Chapter Eight. What you have there in your hands, some of you,
is the synopsis of the first seven chapters. What I'm going to read to you
now is from Chapter Eight. All right? Is that clear? OK. Here we go.
(*Reading*) "Chapter Eight. Inside The Inner Sanctity". That's the subtitle
of the chapter. "Inside The Inner Sanctity" ——
Brevis I think you mean sanctuary, don't you?
Clem What?
Brevis Or possibly sanctum.
Clem No, I don't, I mean sanctity. (*Reading*) "Chapter Eight. Inside The
Inner Sanctity. The two stopped for a moment, listening to the deafening
silence around them. Reaching out with her tentative, slender fingers, Solo
felt she could almost touch the very darkness, so impermeable a blanket did
it present ——"
Brevis Impenetrable.
Clem "—— Then, reassuringly, she heard the sound of Rhona's breathing
beside her and she felt a burden lifted. Still, the nagging question remained
in both their minds — where was Zap? Sandy had been ahead of them for
some way up the stairs but now, inexorably, he had vanished ——"

Brevis Inexplicably. I think you mean inexplicably.

Clem No, I don't. I mean inexorably.

Brevis Doesn't make any sense. Inexplicable meaning without explanation. Inexorably means something quite different. Impossible to stop. Unstoppable.

Clem Right. That'll be you, then?

Vivvi laughs

Brevis I beg your pardon?

Grace Who's Zap, Clem?

Clem What?

Grace Who's this Zap?

Clem Zap's Rex's assistant

Jess Then who on earth's Sandy?

Clem Sandy's Zap.

Jess Sandy is Zap?

Clem (*slightly irritated*) Sandy's his real name. His nickname's Zap. It's all in the synopsis, there. I don't know why everyone's having such trouble. Right. I'll carry on then, all right? (*Reading*) "What to do now? Rhona and Solo were now faced with a predilection ... "

Brevis (*with a mighty yell*) Predicament! A predicament!

Everyone jumps. Vivvi laughs

Arnold Brevis?

Brevis (*rising abruptly*) Dear God, excuse me. I need to use the bathroom. Excuse me.

Brevis goes off towards the kitchen

Clem (*waiting till Brevis has left; imperturbably. Reading*) "What to do now? Rhona and Solo were now faced with a predilection ... "

Grace Sorry, who's Rhona again?

Clem Rhona Reed. She's Rex's assistant.

Jess Then who's Solo?

Clem Solo is also Rex's assistant.

Vivvi Rex?

Clem Rex van Ecks.

Jess How many assistants has he got?

Clem (*exasperated*) Three. There's three of them. Zap, also called Sandy, Solo who hates being called Samantha and Rhona known as Rhona. They're all Rex's assistants. Jesus, how many more times?

Jess Worse than a government department.

Clem Oh, they're not government, Jess. By no means. Quite the reverse. If you'd been listening. It's the government they're investigating.

Arnold Yes, I remember.

Clem Well, the local government. In this chapter they're actually in the town hall itself, I've based it where I work. They're about to break into the Chief Executive's office, in response to an anonymous tip-off which has actually turned out to be a trap. Which explains why Zap has disappeared. He's already been abducted and assimilated along with the Chief Executive himself, who is no longer in control of his own actions.

Jess That I can believe.

Arnold Well, we can't fault you for imagination, Clem. Top prize for that.

Clem I wish it was imagination. In fact, I've altered very little. The truth is all there. Just slanted slightly, to protect myself and those close to me.

Arnold You mean you really did creep into the Chief Executive's office in the middle of the night?

Clem (*significantly*) Let's just say, I am familiar with those who did.

A slight pause

Arnold Yes. Well, I think we must move on now. Fascinating as that is. Good luck, Clem, with the rest of it. We all look forward, I know, to hearing more of the story.

Clem It's only just begun. It's just the beginning, Arnold.

Arnold So, moving on then — Vivvi? I'm sure you've written about three books since we last met, haven't you?

Clem collects up his synopses and puts away his papers under the next

Vivvi Well, you know me, Arnold. Miss Unstoppable. But I am, I really am trying to slow down, I promise. But the stories just keep spilling out of me. Some nights, David says, my boyfriend says, I'm like a woman possessed. Are you ever coming to bed at *all*, woman, you know ... (*She laughs*)

Jess (*who has had enough of this*) I say, do you think Brevis is all right? Sorry to interrupt ...

Arnold Yes, I think he probably is. You know Brevis, he does like to take his time. I think, just between us, he's actually having a spot of trouble with the — the ——

Vivvi Waterworks.

Arnold Not that he'd ever say anything. But you get to that age, don't you? We'll leave him a minute or two more. Don't want to embarrass him.

Vivvi He's got no-one to look after him, poor man. He's missing the love of a good woman, that's his problem.

Grace Good woman? She'd need to be a saint to live with him. (*Confidentially*) His wife left him, you know. Mrs Winterton. She left him ...

Vivvi Yes, there was a rumour ages ago, but ——

Grace It's true. No-one was supposed to know — I was still at the school then, in the sixth form. At the school. It was very hushed up but we all knew. She ran off with a teacher. Another teacher.

Arnold Goodness, I never knew that.

Jess It would explain why he's not very fond of women.

Grace Well, he was never very fond of them. That's why Connie walked out on him. Mrs Winterton. He was horrible to her. Some nights we'd lie awake in the dormitory and we'd hear her crying out from the gym. His wife, you know. Connie Winterton. Wailing. Like an animal. God knows what he was doing to her, poor woman ...

Vivvi Maybe they were both just, you know — having a — (*breaking off*) oh!

Brevis has returned

Vivvi laughs

Arnold Ah, Brevis. Welcome back.

Brevis Have I missed it? Don't tell me I've missed the next chapter?

Clem Yes, you've missed it.

Brevis Oh damn! Damn! Damn! (*He sits*)

Arnold Cheer up, though! You're just in time to hear Vivvi's next instalment.

Brevis She hasn't written another one, has she?

Vivvi Not quite, you'll be relieved to hear.

Brevis She's like Edgar Wallace, she is. Reporter rang up once and said, "May I speak to Edgar Wallace, please?" And his secretary said, "I'm sorry, Mr Wallace is in the middle of writing a book, he's speaking to no-one, I'm afraid." And the reporter said, "That's OK, I'll hang on till he's finished."

Arnold laughs a lot

Vivvi (*laughing*) I'm not as bad as that.

Arnold I'd never heard that before.

Jess I had.

Clem Who's Edgar Wallace, then?

Brevis (*staring at him*) Are you sure you're not an alien, Clem?

Clem Ah, that would be telling. (*He smirks*)

Arnold So. No new novel this month, Vivvi?

Vivvi No, I'm still working on it.

Jess And this will be your — fourth? Fifth?

Vivvi Actually, my sixth.

Jess Sixth. Here's me trying to start on my first.

Vivvi But none of mine are published, Jess. I haven't had any published. They're just lying there, cluttering up the guest bedroom ...

Jess At least they're written. At least you've completed them.

Arnold Your time will come, Jess. Never fear. Who knows? Maybe something will come from this idea of mine. So, Vivvi, can you tell us anything about it, number six? Or is it still shrouded in mystery?

Vivvi It's — it's a bit darker than normal — I've been trying to move into a different area, you know. It's quite surreal some of it.

Arnold Careful. You'll be treading on Clem's territory ...

Vivvi It's still set in the period — vaguely thirties — but I feel the tone of it's quite different. I'm rather excited.

Jess I hope that man's being a bit nicer to his detective sergeant, that's all.

Vivvi DCI Rash? Well, Jim's — Jim's Jim, really. Poor girl, poor Fiona she's passionately in love with him and Jim's immune to her charms.

Jess Doesn't stop him failing in love with practically everyone else.

Vivvi Well, occasionally. It's just, you know, Jim Rash is like lots of men, really. Fiona, his sergeant, she's there all the time so she tends just to get taken for granted.

Jess If you ask me she should get herself transferred.

Vivvi She's tried. She's stood outside the Chief's door twice, the envelope in her hand. But then Jim says something to her, a little bit special, you know, and she just loses the will, poor thing. He is an extraordinarily charismatic man. Such a mind, such sensitivity — on occasions. Adores poetry, of course

Jess Yes, he's forever quoting, isn't he?

Grace Surely if he's that sensitive, doesn't he ever notice his sergeant continually in floods of tears? You'd think he'd notice that, being a detective.

Vivvi He's fixated. Once he's on a case, Jim is fixated. Single track mind. Like most men.

Grace Yes.

Brevis (*roguishly*) I think they're getting at us again, Arnold. The girls are ganging up.

The women glare at him

Vivvi I mean, sometimes I want to reach out and strangle Jim Rash myself for being so — insensitively *masculine* — but then I think, no, I can't. What would happen to poor Fiona then?

Grace She'd be investigating her own boss's death.

Arnold Exactly. So, new book in the offing but nothing yet. Thank you, Vivvi. Now, Jess. Do I gather not a lot more progress?

Jess I've — er — I've been doing a lot more research, you know ... Victorian manners and customs and speech patterns and so on ... I've been reading masses of ... No, I haven't made any progress. Not at all.

Arnold (*gently*) I think you just have to start, Jess ...

Jess I know, I know ...

Arnold ... take a leaf out of Vivvi's book. Jump in with both feet ...

Jess ... I know. I know. That's exactly what that Cataxian man said last month. But you see, at this moment, the book, my book, it's perfect, you see. You know what I'm saying? It's all — there — unsullied. But as soon as I start to write, it will become gradually less perfect. And eventually — I'll have ruined it. Just by writing it, I'll have ruined it. Do you see? Does that make any sense to anyone?

Arnold No, I can't say I follow that at all.

Brevis I think I can.

Arnold How can you ruin something you haven't even written?

Jess Listen, I've said it already. That man was absolutely right. There is no point in me sitting around whingeing and boring the pants off the rest of you. There are lots of people far worse off than me in the world, so stop moaning, Jess, and just get on with it.

Arnold I'll hold you to that, Jess.

Jess You do that.

Arnold And finally — Brevis. Any developments?

Brevis Not really. I'm afraid my absentee collaborator is still failing to deliver.

Arnold No new songs then?

Brevis No new completed songs, certainly. All we've got is a series of half numbers. Most of them trailing off into la-la-la, round about verse two. It's intended to be a through sung show. What's the point of half a song here and half a song there? It's desperately frustrating.

Jess I know we've said it before but it's very ambitious.

Brevis It's not the first musical we've both done, for God's sake. This is our fifth show together, John Chapman and I. All performed, all wildly successful and now suddenly we've hit a rock. I mean *Treasure Island*, the last one John and I did together at the school — at the third and final show — ten curtain calls. Would you believe that, ten.

Arnold Amazing. They don't get that in the West End some nights.

Vivvi Yes, I remember reviewing it for the paper. It was wonderful. All those little pirates with bare chests. Wasn't your son in it, Grace?

Grace Yes ... Delwyn was — yes, he was ... Briefly. He was ill, unfortunately ...

Brevis Delwyn Sims, yes. Walked out after the first show, didn't he? Left us with no bloody Ben Gunn.

Grace He was — he was allergic to the spirit gum. He came out in this terrible ——

Brevis I had to go on instead of him. Little bastards chucking Smarties at me ...

Arnold But no further progress with the new one, Brevis?

Brevis I don't know where the man's got to. I've tried ringing him, leaving messages. I mean, I presume John Chapman's still teaching at the school, he just never seems to be there. Vanished away. Probably found himself a new paramour ...

Vivvi Run off with someone else's wife, probably. (*She laughs. Pause*) Or something.

Arnold So we can't even finish with a song, then? If John hasn't delivered ...

Brevis Well, I suppose we could finish with half a song, if you like.

Arnold (*looking to the others*) Oh yes, half a song's better than none, isn't it?

The others appear doubtful

Brevis (*getting up*) Right. If you all insist, so forcefully. How can I resist? (*He moves to the piano*) This thing's still out of tune, I take it?

Arnold I would imagine so. Mother was always the one who played it, of course. You've never met my mother, have you, Clem?

Clem No.

Arnold No, I think you joined after she was taken ill. We sometimes finished off these meetings with a sing-song, you know. She'd pop in and join us, if she was in the mood. She knew all the old ones.

Brevis (*from behind the piano*) Right. You'll remember this is our own musical take on John Bunyan's *The Pilgrim's Progress* which, for some unaccountable reason, no-one to my knowledge has ever before attempted. This number comes fairly early on when our chum Pilgrim is just setting out on his epic journey. As I say, since it's through sung, this is as much of a stand alone number as we get — or it would be if it had any bloody lyrics — anyway I'll sing you as far as we've got ... (*He plays the brief introduction*)

    (*Singing*) There'll be light at the end of the tunnel.
                Yes, it's bright, have no fear every one'll
                Reach the end, my dear friend,
                As we round that final bend,
                There'll be light! Precious light! There'll be light!
    (*Speaking*) Then, no more lyric ——

(*Singing again*) La-la-la-la-la-la- Cheerio!
         La-la-la-la-la-la- Here I go!
         La-la-la-la-la-la-la-Goodbye.
(*He stops singing*) Etc. Etc. That's your lot. End of lyric.

The others applaud

Thank you. (*Awkwardly, rising*) Excuse me, I ... if I may, Arnold ...
Arnold Help yourself, Brevis.

Brevis goes off towards the kitchen again

Well. I think that concludes the meeting, really. I hereby declare it closed.

Grace rises immediately and gets her coat

Oh yes, next meeting — when did we agree?
Vivvi (*also rising*) January twenty-third.

Clem also starts to gather up his things

Arnold Yes, that's right. January twenty-third. I have that in my diary.
Jess I may not be able to make that one, Arnold. I'll have to let you know.
Arnold No, well, let me know nearer the time, Jess, if you can, that'll be
    lovely. In any event, I still expect you to have started by then ...
Jess New Year resolution.
Arnold That's the spirit.
Grace Arnold, forgive me, I'm going to run for the earlier bus. There's one
    due in about three minutes. I might just catch it.
Arnold Yes, of course, off you go, Grace, off you go.
Grace (*opening the front door*) 'Night all!!
Everyone 'Night!

Grace goes out

Vivvi (*buttoning her coat; to Clem*) Are you ready, then?
Clem I'm ready.
Vivvi We'll be off too, then. Got a date with David later.
Arnold Oh, don't be late for David. Mustn't keep the boyfriend waiting.
Vivvi I don't know why not, he's always doing it to me. (*She laughs*)
Jess Still the same one then, is it?
Vivvi (*defensively*) What do you mean? It has been for ages. David. Has been
    for months. Well, weeks and weeks, anyway. Say good-bye to Brevis for
    me, will you?

Arnold Will do.
Vivvi 'Bye!

Vivvi goes out

Clem (*following her*) 'Night.
Arnold 'Night, Clem.
Jess Good-night.

Clem goes out, closing the door

Arnold Ah, well, meeting suddenly over.
Jess (*awkwardly*) Arnold, I didn't want to say this in front of the others but
if for some reason I can't get started on this bloody book ... Well,
increasingly, I'm feeling a dreadful fraud. I mean, there's people like Vivvi
and Paula — Bernard and Gerald — they really stick at it, don't they? Even
Clem. They're sort of professionals, aren't they? Then there's people like
me, we're just — playing at it.
Arnold You said yourself it has to be fun. Don't give up, Jess.
Jess Sheer waste of space, really. Well, we'll see.
Arnold See how you get on, eh?

Brevis returns, clearing his throat. He stops by the piano

Jess (*sotto*) And frankly, I'm not sure how much more I can take of that old
bugger, either.
Arnold (*sotto*) Oh, you mustn't mind him. I wouldn't be surprised if he
chucks it all in before much longer.
Jess I doubt that somehow. (*Louder*) Good-night then, Arnold.
Arnold Good-night, Jess.
Jess (*calling back to Brevis*) 'Night, Brevis.
Brevis 'Night.

Jess goes out

(*Still at the piano*) You need to get this thing tuned, you know.
Arnold Yes, I know, I ——
Brevis It's actually not a bad piano. But if you don't tune it fairly soon, it'll
be a lost cause. Anyway. I'll be off. Thanks for the coffee. (*He starts to put
on his coat*)
Arnold My pleasure. Very good that new one, Brevis. Good tune. Catchy.
Makes a nice contrast to the others. Bit more upbeat ...
Brevis Yes, difficult to be upbeat writing about The Slough of Despond, of
course. Right, I'll be off then. Hope no-one's been at my bike again.

Arnold I shouldn't think so. Not out here.
Brevis You're a good bloke, you know, Arnold.
Arnold (*flattered*) Oh. Thank you, Brevis.
Brevis Very good bloke. You deserve better, you really do.
Arnold Do I? Better than what?
Brevis Better than us lot, for a kick off. God, it's freezing. 'night, 'night.
Arnold 'Bye.

Brevis goes out, closing the front door

Well. Early night, I think. (*He moves to start gathering up the odd cup*)

In a moment Ilsa appears at the top of the stairs

Oh, hallo there.
Ilsa I heard them all going. Here, I'll give you a hand with those.
Arnold No, no, I'll do them.
Ilsa Finished early, didn't you? Kev won't be here to pick me up for a bit.
Time to wash up, if you want.
Arnold No, Ilsa, you don't need to wash up now ...
Ilsa (*grabbing the tray and heading for the kitchen*) No, I'd like to wash up.
It's OK. Your mum's asleep ...

Ilsa goes off to the kitchen

Arnold (*to himself*) She really doesn't need to wash up ...

A rumble of thunder

Oh, that doesn't sound so good

Arnold picks up a couple of the dining-room chairs and takes them off. He returns

More thunder, louder

(*Looking up*) I hope this doesn't wake her up. She won't like this. (*Calling to the kitchen*) You all right there, are you, Ilsa?
Ilsa (*off*) Yes. Did you hear that thunder?
Arnold (*calling*) Yes, I did. The sooner we get you home the better.

Arnold starts to tidy the other furniture. He picks up another two dining-room chairs and starts for the dining-room again. He leaves the room

There is another much louder clap of thunder

Quite suddenly all the lights go out. There is a crash from the dining-room as Arnold is plunged into the dark

(*From the darkness; off*) Oh, no. Oh dear, oh dear! That's all we need.

We hear, rather than see, Arnold returning to the room

(*As he enters, calling*) Ilsa! Ilsa! Are you all right? Ilsa? (*He listens. Calling*) Listen, Ilsa. If you're still in the kitchen ... You'll find some candles in the left hand cupboard under the sink ... Can you find them? Ilsa? (*He listens*) Hang on. I'll come and help you. If I can see the way.

There is a glow of candlelight from the kitchen as Ilsa approaches the door

Oh, good girl. You found them. Well done.

Ilsa enters. She carries a single candlestick and in the other hand, as yet unseen, a large, wicked-looking, old-fashioned kitchen knife. She is now wearing a Victorian dress. Her appearance has also altered

Ilsa? (*He stares at her, confused*) Ilsa — what's ...

We see the knife in Ilsa's hand. She is breathing heavily. She stops, facing Arnold in the middle of the room

(*Somewhat alarmed*) Ilsa ... what on earth are you doing?

From the top of the stairs comes more light as Dr Thomas Goodpiece (Brevis) appears with an impressive three-pronged candelabra. The area brightens slightly

Simultaneously:

Mrs Dimchurch (Vivvi), the housekeeper, and Mrs Boon (Grace), the cook, enter together from the kitchen

Miss Norris (Jess), the tutor, enters from the direction of the dining-room

Dudley Carstairs (Clem), dressed for riding, enters through the front door

They all stand in this tableau for a second. Then Ilsa, looking round at them all, suddenly screams loudly

Arnold, looking around, too, also feels a bit like screaming. Instead he says:

  Good gracious!

Black-out

ACT II

The same. A few seconds before

Darkness. Everyone is in the same positions as they were at the end of ACT I. The phone is no longer there

Ilsa's scream is heard again in the darkness

Arnold (*from the darkness*) Good gracious.

The Lights come up. The room is lit by candlelight, though now there is also a light on Miss Norris (Jess), the tutor, and narrator for all the Victorian sections

Jess (*as Miss Norris*) For a brief moment, following the distraught girl's piercing scream, there reigned a deathly silence. The entire household was now assembled in the hall, summoned by the commotion. We stood, motionless, uncertain as to whom should make the first movement. At the top of the stairs stood the imposing figure of Dr Thomas Goodpiece, physician and long term friend of the Hassock family; across the hall, having hurried from below stairs, stood Mrs Dimchurch, the housekeeper, together with Mrs Boon, the cook; and there, lounging in the front doorway, the nephew, Dudley Carstairs, that familiar half-smile, half-sneer playing on his thin lips. And finally, I, Elizabeth Norris, spinster, recently employed by the Hassocks' as tutor to Miss Ilsa, their adopted ward. Upon hearing the disturbance, I had, myself, hurried from the drawing-room. The sight that confronted me was indeed alarming. Dear kindly Mr Hassock stood confused, a frown of bewilderment furrowing his customarily benign features, menaced as he was by the very child he had adopted as his own when she was but a few hours old; that same girl he had rescued from the cold, grey prison of an orphanage, and welcomed into the warmth and colour of his own home. As for Ilsa, the long kitchen knife still in her hand, she too seemed uncertain now, staring about her as if unsure of her surroundings or of how she had even come to be there. Thus we stood, for those endless seconds before Dr Goodpiece finally broke the silence.

Brevis (*as Dr Goodpiece, gently*) Put down the knife, child.

Ilsa hesitates

(*Still calmly*) Ilsa. No-one means you harm, child. Please, put down the
knife.

Ilsa, after a second, puts it down. The others relax slightly

Brevis (*descending the stairs*) Thank you, Ilsa. May I suggest, Mrs Boon,
you kindly return to your kitchen replacing if you would that kitchen knife
where it belongs?
Grace (*as Mrs Boon*) Yes, Doctor.

Grace picks up the knife rather gingerly and goes off to the kitchen

Brevis (*turning to Jess*) Miss Norris, I fear you have been dreadfully
disturbed. My apologies. Please, be assured all is now in hand. You may
safely return to your reading.
Jess Thank you, Doctor. (*To us*) But I did not go back to the drawing room.
Rather, I made to leave but instead held back in the shadows, anxious to
learn more of these events.
Arnold Are you all right, Ilsa?
Brevis Please, Arnold, dear friend. Allow me to speak to her. Ilsa, my
child ——
Ilsa (*with no trace of an accent*) Doctor?
Brevis What caused this, child? What is the reason for this wild and
disturbing behaviour? Can you account for it?
Ilsa (*falteringly*) I — I ... I cannot tell, I ...
Brevis Understand this, Ilsa, you have threatened those who love you. Why
should you wish to do this?
Ilsa I — I hear voices ...
Brevis Voices? What voices are these?
Ilsa In the night. When I am asleep, I wake and there are voices ... And at other
times ... Whenever I am alone. Walking. Or at my studies ...
Brevis And what do they say to you, these voices, do you recollect?
Ilsa That I — I am unworthy and unloved. That I have no right to be here.
I defile this beautiful home by my presence. That I belong in the gutter.
Arnold Oh, come now ...
Clem (*as Dudley*) The girl is quite deranged.
Brevis One moment, Dudley ——
Clem Clearly she deserves to be certified, Doctor.
Arnold Certified? What are you talking about?
Brevis Arnold, my friend! Please. (*To Ilsa*) Go on, child. What else? What
caused you to take that knife?

Ilsa I saw — a face ——
Brevis A face? What face?
Ilsa Just now. At the kitchen window ... cruel ... twisted ... mocking me ...
Brevis Did anyone else witness this?
Ilsa No, they were ... busy ... they ...

Brevis looks at Vivvi

Vivvi *(as Mrs Dimchurch)* None of us saw anything, sir.
Ilsa You don't believe me, do you? None of you believe me ... *(Weeping)*
Oh, what is to become of me? Am I truly losing my reason?
Arnold I believe you, Ilsa.
Brevis Child, we both believe you. At least, we believe that *you* see and hear
these things and we are merely anxious to ascertain their cause ——
Ilsa I knew! I knew it! *(Turning to Arnold)* I am sorry, dear guardian. I have
failed you! Will you ever forgive me, Uncle? *(Weeping, she throws herself
at Arnold and embraces him, sobbing into his chest, clasping him. Muffled)*
Forgive me! Forgive me! Forgive me!
Arnold Oh, dear! Come, now ...

During Jess's following speech, Brevis gently prises Ilsa away from Arnold

Jess *(to us)* At the sight of this heart-breaking spectacle, my first thought was
to rush forward and clasp the poor girl and comfort her, for truth be told,
in those few weeks I had been in service at Hassock Hall, I had grown
inordinately fond of her. However, before I could do so ...
Brevis Mrs Dimchurch, would you be so good as to take Miss Ilsa to her room
and sit with her until I am able to join you?
Vivvi Yes, doctor. Come along, Miss Ilsa ...

Vivvi takes Ilsa gently by the elbow and guides her up the stairs

Brevis I will be there shortly. I will prepare a draught to help her to sleep.

Vivvi and Ilsa go off upstairs

(Urgently) Arnold, my friend, we must talk together ...
Arnold Yes?
Brevis *(with a glance at Clem)* Alone.
Clem Uncle — excuse me, Doctor — I wonder if I could crave the loan of
a sovereign or two ...
Arnold A sovereign? Well ...

Clem I find myself at present unexpectedly impoverished until my allowance
is paid at the end of the month.

Arnold I don't know that I've got anything like a sovereign. Fifty p, is that
any ——?

Brevis Permit me, Arnold. Here, half a sovereign, that is all we can give you.

Clem Half a sovereign!

Brevis Whatever the sum, I presume you will drink it away in no time
at all ...

Clem Half a sovereign will scarcely quench my thirst ——

Brevis That is all, do you hear? Now go, before I change my mind!

Clem (*heading for the front door; angrily*) It has come to a pretty pass, has
it not, when a rightful heir is denied what is his!

Clem goes out of the front door

Brevis Miserable fellow. Forgive me, Arnold, I know he is your nephew
but I confess I have never taken to the fellow — gambling, drinking,
whoring ...

Arnold No, well, he has his good side, I don't think we should ...

Brevis (*clasping Arnold's elbow; affectionately*) Dear Arnold! Ever the
trusting soul, ready to forgive. However, I think the girl, Ilsa, is another
matter. As you have seen, she is, daily, growing increasingly disturbed and
now these hallucinations ...

Arnold You think they're hallucinations?

Brevis Oh, decidedly. They clearly have no substance. But, importantly, I
fear for you, my friend.

Arnold Me?

Brevis Could you doubt just now that she intended you harm?

Arnold Oh, never! Not Ilsa!

Brevis Arnold, dear friend, I have delayed telling you this but I fear for you
both. For you and your sister.

Arnold My sister? I don't have a sister ——

Brevis Very nearly not, my friend. It was a close run thing but I believe I have
saved her. Arnold, I fear, though, she was almost certainly poisoned.

Arnold Poisoned? Who was poisoned?

Brevis Elaine, man! Your sister, Elaine.

Arnold Elaine? That's my mother!

Brevis Dear fellow, please contain yourself. I could not bear for anything to
happen to you. Your mind must remain strong ——

Arnold My mother ...

Brevis Your sister is resting now. But I suspect poisoning by laudanum. She
was displaying classic symptoms ...

Arnold (*heading for the stairs; alarmed*) Oh, good gracious.

Brevis (*grasping his arm and stopping him*) Please, Arnold, dear fellow! I say, she is resting. Leave her, I beg you. You may see her later. I promise, she will shortly recover.

Arnold Listen, if she's ill I should phone. I need to phone. (*Examining the sideboard*) Where's the phone gone?

Brevis Arnold, pay attention, I fear the girl is responsible. As the hours go by, her mind is becoming increasingly unhinged and dangerous ...

Arnold No, she won't have taken it. What's happened to the phone?

Brevis Listen, only yesterday Mrs Dimchurch discovered her, the child Ilsa, lowering the new-born kittens into the well ...

Arnold She did? What kittens?

Brevis The girl claimed to be rescuing them but ... Fortunately, Mrs Dimchurch ... Arnold, I am so sorry. You, of all people, to experience such tragedy. A girl, upon whom you and your sister lavished their love ... How must you be feeling ...

Arnold A bit confused, actually ...

Brevis Dear friend, be assured I will do whatever I can. But it may be that, despite all our best efforts, the girl will need to be locked away, for her own safety as well as yours. (*He moves to the stairs*) I must see to her now. Prepare a draught to allow her poor fevered brain some blessed relief through sleep. Courage, dear fellow!

Brevis goes off upstairs

Arnold stares up the stairs after Brevis, startled

Jess (*to us*) Upon witnessing this and the now solitary figure of Mr Hassock so lonely and seemingly betrayed by those he loved, I risked all and stepped forward to speak to him. (*To Arnold*) Mr Hassock ...

Arnold Ah! Oh hallo, Jess. Listen, what's going on, do you ... ?

Jess (*urgently*) Mr Hassock, please hear me! I know I am a newcomer to your household ... But, in the space of these past few weeks, I have grown close enough to your niece to become privy to many of her inmost thoughts. I can assure you, Mr Hassock, as God is my witness, that child is no more mad or deranged, no more a murderer ——

A loud knock on the front door

I must go, forgive me. I beg you, Mr Hassock, to remember my words. (*She hurries away. As she goes: to us*) I feared the knocking presaged the return of Dudley and I was anxious to say no more in front of him ...

Jess goes out towards the dining-room leaving Arnold alone

Thunder

The Lights change. It is now daylight in the room with sun streaming through the windows. An old-fashioned candlestick phone has now appeared on the sideboard

Arnold (*confused*) What —— ?

The doorbell rings. It is a different doorbell from normal

What's that, then?

The doorbell rings again, more impatiently

Is that a doorbell? That's not my doorbell. What's going on? (*He opens the front door rather cautiously*)

Standing there are DCI Jim Rash (Clem) and DS Fiona Longstaff (Vivvi)

Clem (*as Jim Rash*) Good-morning, sir.
Arnold Good-morning. Is it?
Clem Mr Hassock?
Arnold (*cautiously*) Yes.
Clem May we come in? Detective Chief Inspector Jim Rash, and this is Detective Sergeant Longstaff.
Vivvi (*as Fiona*) How d'you do, sir.
Arnold Oh! Well, now! Good gracious! Heavens ...
Clem May we come in?
Arnold Yes, of course. I — Come in. You know, this is quite extraordinary! You know, Vivvi, I thought you made them up — I had no idea — well, yes, you did make them up, didn't you? That's Clem, isn't it? That's not — is it? That's Clem ——
Clem No, it's not Clem. It's Jim, sir.
Arnold Jim?
Clem Jim Rash. DCI.
Arnold And that's not Vivvi.
Clem No, that's DS Longstaff, sir.
Arnold Longstaff?
Vivvi Fiona Longstaff.
Arnold Yes ... Excuse me, I ...

Vivvi You all right, are you, sir?

Arnold Yes, I just feel a — a — a trifle dizzy. I may have missed a bit of sleep somewhere. I'm not quite sure.

Vivvi Perhaps you'd care to sit down, sir.

Arnold Yes, maybe I — maybe I should ... Actually, I'm secretly hoping that I might wake up in a minute. (*He sits*)

Clem I won't beat about the bush, sir. Earlier this morning, we received an anonymous phone call reporting a suspicious death. That call was subsequently traced to this house.

Arnold This house?

Clem (*rather smugly*) We're capable of doing that these days, sir.

Arnold Well, you can't have traced it here.

Vivvi Why not?

Arnold We haven't got a phone. Someone appears to have stolen our phone.

Vivvi Really? What's that then?

Arnold What?

Vivvi Over there.

Arnold (*looking towards the sideboard*) Oh. That's — that's not my phone.

Clem Really? Well it's plugged into your wall, sir. Standing on your sideboard. In your house. I presume this is your house?

Arnold Yes, of course it's my house!

Vivvi Which is jointly owned by you and your wife, Mrs Hassock?

Arnold I haven't got a wife!

Clem No, not any more you don't.

Arnold What?

Clem Not if that phone call was anything to go by.

Arnold What are you talking about?

Vivvi (*getting a little aggressive*) I think you know, Mr Hassock. I think you know very well what we're ——

Clem (*sharply and quietly to her*) All right, Sergeant, that's enough of that!

Vivvi (*meekly*) Yes, sir.

Ilsa appears at the top of the stairs. She is now dressed in a 1930s housemaid's outfit. She is very sniffly and tearful

Clem Hallo, who have we here ...?

Arnold Ilsa!

Ilsa (*in a different accent to her normal one*) Oh, Mr Hassock! Oh, sir ... (*She hurries down the stairs*)

Arnold Ilsa, what's the matter now ...?

Ilsa Oh, sir, the mistress is dead. I can't bear to think of her, lying there dead. What are we to do, sir?

Clem "When she I loved looked every day, Fresh as a rose in June ..." This'll be your maid, I take it?

Arnold I take it it is, yes.
Vivvi (*rather beadily*) We'll need to question her later.
Clem So there has been a death, then?
Arnold No, there's not been a death.
Ilsa She's dead, sir.
Vivvi There has been a death.
Arnold (*excitedly*) Listen, there's not been a death. There's been no death. I have no wife, there's been no death, do you hear?

Mavis Green (Grace) appears at the top of the stairs

Grace (*as Mavis*) Oh, yes, there has.

They all look up at her

Clem And who might you be, madam?
Grace I am the sister of the deceased. My name is Green. Miss Mavis Green. I am Elaine's sister.
Arnold *Elaine's* sister. You mean Enid? Enid's been dead for years.
Grace My sister died earlier this morning. The maid there discovered her dead in bed. The doctor has already been. He has signed the certificate declaring death by natural causes.
Clem Then I'm not sure why this concerns the police, madam ...
Grace I telephoned you because I am not satisfied. I suspect that it was far from natural causes.
Clem I see. And have you any reason for those suspicions?
Grace (*with a glance at Arnold and Ilsa*) Several.
Vivvi Would you care to share them with us?
Grace Not — in present company, no, I would not.
Clem I see. Well, I think we should take a look for ourselves, don't you, Sergeant? (*To Grace*) "Like the touch of rain she was, On a man's flesh and hair and eyes ..." Would you care to lead on, madam?
Grace Yes, of course.

Grace leads Clem and Vivvi up the stairs

Arnold (*making to follow*) Right.
Clem No. You stay down here, sir, if you don't mind.
Arnold But it's my mother, I mean, if she's really ——
Clem We're not worried about your mother, sir, not at present. I'm sure your mother's fine. It's your wife we're concerned with at present.
Arnold For the tenth time, I don't have a wife!
Vivvi We're well aware of that, sir. Don't leave the house!

Grace goes off at the top of the stairs

Clem and Vivvi linger for a quick exchange

Clem (*softly to Vivvi*) Sergeant, in future you will allow me to do the questioning without further interruptions from you, all right?
Vivvi Sir.
Clem I can do without you chiming in every ten seconds. In future, you take your notes and hold your tongue. I won't tell you again.
Vivvi (*in a little voice*) Yes, sir.

Clem goes off upstairs after Grace

Vivvi's face crumples as she fights back tears. She follows them off

Arnold Ilsa, what on earth is going on? First you're this, then you're that ...
Ilsa Oh, sir ...
Arnold First it's evening, then it's morning ...
Ilsa It was nothing to do with me, sir, I swear it!
Arnold Someone keeps swapping the phones around ... What's nothing to do with you?
Ilsa Mrs Hassock's death, sir. I swear it. But I know they're going to suspect me, whatever.
Arnold Why should they suspect you, for goodness sake?
Ilsa Because I had a motive, sir, I have a motive ...
Arnold What motive?
Ilsa When I went in to wake Mrs Hassock this morning and I saw her lying there all crumpled and dead, I confess it, sir, I felt joy in my heart. I know it was sinful but that's what I felt.
Arnold But why?
Ilsa There's no stronger motive in the world, is there, sir? Not in the whole wide world, there isn't. Isn't that what they say?
Arnold What motive? What are you talking about?
Ilsa Love, sir.
Arnold Love?
Ilsa Our love. Yours and mine.
Arnold What on earth are you talking about?
Ilsa Sssh! They're coming back. (*Sotto*) I'll love you for ever. Even if they send me to the gallows, I'll love you.

Clem and Vivvi enter at the top of the stairs

Clem What's that?

Arnold Nothing.

Clem "The flowers join lips below; the leaves above; And every sound that meets the ear is love." (*He descends the stairs*) For what it's worth, it's my belief your wife died by another's hand. In other words, she was murdered. She had clearly fallen asleep, having read for a while. Her book was by the bed along with her glasses. I understand she wore glasses in normal circumstances, is that correct, sir?

Arnold I haven't the faintest idea.

Clem gives Vivvi a look during the following

Vivvi It would be in your interest to co-oper— (*Breaking off at Clem's look*) Sorry, sir.

Clem As my sergeant was about to say, it would be in your best interest to try to co-operate, sir. The police don't particularly warm to obstruction.

Arnold (*uncertain how to answer*) — Er ...

Ilsa Mrs Hassock wore glasses all the time. Every day.

Clem Thank you, girl. Well done. No, my deduction is that the deceased fell asleep and that persons, as yet unknown, during the night crept in and smothered her with her own pillow.

Arnold Oh, dear. (*He looks at Ilsa*)

Ilsa (*softly, to him*) It wasn't me.

Clem You, girl!

Ilsa (*jumping*) Sir?

Clem Summon the household. I want everyone assembled in this room in five minutes, do you hear?

Ilsa Yes, sir.

Ilsa hurries out towards the kitchen

Clem And I'd be obliged, sir, if you didn't move from there.

Arnold Right. Just as you like.

Clem I'm just going to have a look outside, Sergeant. Check the window ledges and the flower beds.

Vivvi Yes, sir. (*She sniffs*)

Clem I'm almost convinced it's an inside job but we need to make doubly ... Something the matter, Sergeant?

Vivvi (*tearfully*) Nothing, sir. Just a touch of — hay fever ...

Clem Well, you'd better stay here indoors, hadn't you? Can't have you tramping around the flower beds, can we? I'll go on my own.

Vivvi (*miserably*) No, sir. I'll come with you.

Clem (*heading out*) Suit yourself, Sergeant.

Clem exits. Vivvi, after another sob, follows him

*The Lights dip and re-establish. It is night again, similar — but not quite the
same — as it was at the start of the play. Arnold's original phone is back in
place*

Arnold (*as this happens*) Oh, not again. Ah! Back to normal, thank
goodness!

The "normal" doorbell rings, confirming this

Oh, good. That'll be Kev. Come to collect Ilsa. (*Calling towards the
kitchen*) Ilsa! (*He opens the door*)

*It is Rex van Ecks (Brevis), investigator, with one of his glamorous
assistants, Rhona Reed (Grace)*

(*Opening the door*) Hallo, Kevin, you're just in ——
Brevis (*as Rex, marching in without ceremony*) Hi! Rex van Ecks, you must
be Arnie.
Arnold Sorry?
Brevis Rex van Ecks. Paranormal investigator. My assistant, Rhona Reed.
Grace (*as Rhona*) Hi! Call me Rhona.
Brevis Now, Arnie, we're working against the clock here. I need to cut
through the shit, OK? You with me on this?
Arnold — Er ——
Grace Where did it all happen?
Arnold Where did what happen?
Brevis The abduction, where did it happen?
Arnold Abduction? I've no idea ——
Brevis Arnie, Arnie, stay with us, please ——
Grace Don't lose us, baby. I know it's hard ...
Brevis If we mean to find her, we have to move with the greatest
expeditiousness, you follow?
Arnold With the what?
Grace — We can't hang around ——
Brevis — the longer we wait ——
Grace — the more they'll do to her.
Arnold Do to who? You mean Ilsa?
Grace Arnie, your mother, baby. We're talking about your mother.
Arnold My mother?
Brevis Look at me, Arnie. Your mother. Remember her, your mother!
Arnold (*bounding up*) My mother's been abducted?
Grace Arnie!

Arnold heads for the stairs

Brevis (*urgently*) Stop him, Rhona!

Grace springs across the room, grabs Arnold and armlocks him into the chair

Arnold Ow! Ow! Ow!
Grace (*depositing him*) Sorry, baby.
Brevis We're going up to look, Arnie. You stay right there.
Arnold Ow!

Brevis and Grace climb the stairs

Brevis (*as they go*) Take my advice, Arnie, don't tangle with Rhona. Never tangle again with Rhona. She's insalubrious. She doesn't know her own strength. Back soon.

Brevis goes off upstairs

Grace (*following Brevis; to Arnold*) I'd never hurt you, not really, baby.

Grace exits

Arnold What do you mean, you just have! I'm being assaulted now.

More thunder. The Lights change, the phone vanishes

The front door slams open. It is Clem, as Dudley, now very drunk

Simultaneously Jess, as Miss Norris, appears in the dining-room doorway. A light comes up on her. As she sees Clem, she draws back

Clem (*as Dudley; drunkenly*) Well, well, well! Good-evening, Uncle!
Arnold Oh, it's you again.
Clem Me, again. Like a bad penny, Uncle ... (*He lurches towards the stairs*)
Jess (*as Miss Norris; to us*) I entered the hallway in time to witness Dudley's drunken return, presumably from the village alehouse. Even from my concealed vantage point, I could tell that the man reeked of stale ale and cheap perfume, the kind only worn by the lowest, most depraved type of woman.
Clem And how fares my sweet cousin? Poor little Ilsa. By the way, Uncle, I have given instructions — for the safety of us all — I have instructed the housekeeper, Mrs Dimchurch, to lock the sorry creature in the cellar overnight.
Arnold In the cellar?

Clem Maybe the rats can convince her of the folly of her ways. Poor Ilsa, she'll surely hang; surely she'll hang. Along with all her inheritance ... Isn't that the saddest thing, Uncle dear ...?

Clem goes off upstairs

Jess Suddenly, the very depths of Dudley's evil plan were clear to me. But what was I to do? I, a mere governess? What could I possibly do?

Jess goes off back to the dining-room

Arnold We haven't got a cellar.

The Lights change to the modern setting. The modern phone reappears

Rex (Brevis) and Rhona (Grace) enter and come downstairs again

Brevis (*as Rex, descending the stairs*) Right, Arnie, this is the situation. Your mother's ostentatiously been taken, her bed's empty ——
Grace — I'm so sorry, baby ——
Brevis — they've certainly been there, the room is covered in spores ——
Grace — the sheets, the bedding ——
Brevis — everywhere ——
Grace — you don't want to see it — they're umbiquitous.
Arnold What?
Brevis However, the good news, let's give you the good news, Arnie ...
Arnold Please ...
Brevis We had a message just now from my base. It appears they left one behind. One of their own.
Grace You following this, baby ...?
Brevis Which means somewhere, very close by, there's one of them ...
Grace A live alien ...
Brevis ... living, breathing, sententious ... somewhere close by ...
Grace You follow?
Arnold (*humouring them, as best he can*) Yes, I'll keep a look out then, shall I?
Brevis Arnie, don't even bother. These people, you'd never recognize them. They assume human form ——
Grace — they transmographize — like that ——
Brevis — just like that. (*To Grace*) Rhona, call Solo and Zap. We need some STJ's here ——
Grace How many?
Brevis Six in here, the rest outside.

Grace You got it.
Brevis And an X5TR 77.
Grace Check. An X5TR 77.
Brevis Make sure it's a seven. I don't want a six, it wouldn't be congenial.
Grace Seven. Check. Anything else?
Brevis Well ... (*With a rare smile*) I could do with a little hot soup.
Grace (*smiling*) Hot soup it is, chief.

Grace goes out

Brevis (*calling after her, affectionately*) Go! Go! Go! Rhona! (*To Arnold*) What we plan to do, Arnie, we're going to place sensors all around the area. This way, if anything alien passes within eight feet of them — pow — gotcha!
Arnold You mean you're going to kill them?
Brevis Kill them, no. Hell, capture. Capture them. Catch this stray, you realize it'll be the first time we've ever had one in our hands? In twenty years? A live alien. Can you believe that? They're clever, Arnie, cleverer than us but they're not involatable. They've taken over, they can still make mistakes. Even in the town hall, they make mistakes. Back soon. Don't have dreams, don't talk to strangers, OK?

Brevis goes

Arnold They're getting madder by the minute. What have they done with my mother? (*He moves to the stairs*)

As he does so, the Lights change to the Victorian settings, the phone vanishes and there is more thunder

Mrs Dimchurch (Vivvi) appears on the stairs, dragging Ilsa by the wrist, heading down the stairs and towards the kitchen. Miss Norris (Jess) appears in the dining-room doorway and a light comes up on her

Ilsa (*weakly protesting*) ... No ... no ... please ...
Vivvi (*as Mrs Dimchurch*) Come along, Miss Ilsa. Master's orders, now ...
Ilsa ... Not in the cellar ... please, Mrs. Dimchurch ... not in the cellar ..
Vivvi It won't do you any good to struggle, Miss Ilsa ...
Jess (*as Miss Norris, to us*) I watched helplessly. Was there nothing I could do to help her?
Ilsa ... Not in the darkness ... whatever else, not in the dark ... (*To Arnold*) Oh, dearest uncle, help me, please ...!

Arnold Now, listen, what do you think you're doing, Mrs — er ...?

Ilsa and Vivvi exit into the kitchen

Jess (*to us*) There was nothing I could do ...
Arnold (*with sudden determination*) Oh, yes, there was. I'm sorry, I'm not having this. I'm putting a stop to this ...

Jess goes off

Arnold moves resolutely towards the kitchen. Before he gets far, the Lights change again to daylight, the candlestick phone appears and, as this happens, the front door swings open

DCI Rash (Clem) enters, closing the door behind him

Now what ——?
Clem (*as Rash*) Off somewhere, were you, Mr Hassock?
Arnold Yes, I was, as a matter of fact, I was ——
Clem I'd be grateful if you could hang on here a few moments more, sir. My sergeant is just rounding up the household. I'm requesting them all to assemble in here. I have a few general questions I wish to ask.
Arnold So have I.
Clem You turn will come, Mr Hassock, I promise you. Be it in the witness box or be it in the dock.
Arnold (*alarmed*) The dock?
Clem All in good time.

Mavis (Grace) appears on the stairs. She is carrying a handbag

Ah, Miss Green, thank you for finding the time to join us.
Grace (*as Mavis*) What's happened? Have you discovered the perpetrator?
Clem Not quite yet, Miss Green. But I'm getting there. Please, come down.

The front door opens and Run Cater (Brevis) the gardener enters

Ah, who would this be?
Grace That's — that is the gardener, I believe, — er ——
Brevis (*as Run*) Run.
Clem Sorry?
Brevis Run Cater. Ilsa's dad.
Clem Ah, you're the girl's father. It falls into place.
Brevis She's a good girl.

Clem Possibly. Do come in and close the door, Ron.
Brevis (*closing the door*) Run.
Clem Run.

Ilsa and Connie Cater (Jess), the cook, enter from the kitchen. Behind them is Fiona (Vivvi)

Come along in, then. Is that the lot, Sergeant?
Vivvi (*as Fiona*) Yes. This is Mrs Cater, Ilsa's mother ——
Clem Yes, I had already gathered that, Sergeant, thank you for pointing it out. Do sit down everyone — Mrs Cater ...
Jess (*as Connie*) I'm not sitting down, not in here.
Clem Just as you wish.

They all remain standing

Now, as to the reason I've summoned you. Miss Green — (*smiling at her*) Mavis — has shown me a very interesting letter. A letter written ——

An involuntary sob from Vivvi

— do be quiet, Sergeant — a letter written to her by her late sister, Elaine, a few days before she died. In it, she invites Miss Green to visit her, here at Hollyhock Cottage. However, the really interesting feature of the letter is the urgency of its tone. (*He produces the letter from his pocket*) I wonder if you would be so good as to read it to us, Miss Green.
Grace Me? Oh well, yes, of course. (*Fumbling in her handbag*) One moment — I'll need my — (*finding her glasses*) — ah! Forever mislaying the things ... Now then.

Clem hands Grace the letter

Thank you. (*Staring at the letter*) Oh — oh, dear ...
Clem A problem?
Grace (*holding the letter at various distances from her face*) No, no. Just these wretched reading glasses. I really need a new prescription but ... (*Reading with difficulty, or perhaps it is from memory*) "My dear Mavis, Please come and visit me as soon as you can. It is the matter of the most urgency. I have reason to believe that someone is trying to kill me. Hurry, please. Your loving sister, Elaine." (*She removes her glasses and puts them down on a table*)
Clem (*taking back the letter*) Thank you, Miss Green. Well, now. Isn't that interesting? What do we all make of that, then?

A silence. Then, with a cry, Ilsa makes a dash for the front door

Ilsa (*as she does so*) It wasn't me! I tell you, it wasn't me!
Vivvi Come back, you!
Brevis Ilsa!
Jess Ilsa! Come back here!

Ilsa throws open the front door and dashes out. Brevis and Jess follow her, calling her name, closing the door behind them

Fiona moves to pursue them but is too late

During this, unseen by the others, Clem picks up Grace's glasses and slips them into his pocket

Clem Well, that seems to have cleared the room of suspects, Sergeant. Well done.
Vivvi Sorry, sir.
Clem Don't worry, they're not going far. We'll catch up with her. (*He moves to the front door*) Did your sister say anything else to you, Miss Green? I mean, in person? Did she elaborate on this letter when you saw her?
Grace No, that's the point. I never saw her.
Clem You didn't?
Grace By the time I arrived last night Elaine had already retired to bed. The wretched trains were completely haywire, as usual. And then by this morning, of course ...
Clem Of course.
Arnold Are you going to charge Ilsa with murder?
Clem (*turning*) Do you know, I don't think I am. I've changed my mind.
Grace You have? Why on earth is that?
Clem I think the girl may possibly be implicated but I very much doubt that she's responsible. I feel we need to widen our search a little if we wish to catch the guilty ones. (*Opening the door and admiring the view*) Beautiful! "The Spring comes in with all her hues and smells, In freshness breathing over hills and dells ..."

Clem exits through the front door, passing Vivvi

Vivvi (*to them, after Clem has gone; tearfully*) Isn't he just wonderful?

Vivvi goes out and closes the front door

Arnold Well, despite everything this is getting quite enthralling. I wonder who did it. It can't be Ilsa, he's right. She's far too obvious. I wonder who he thinks did it? Have you any idea?

Grace I've no idea at all, Arnold. Who knows? Possibly you.

Arnold Me? Good heavens. I don't even know the woman.

Grace How typical of you, Arnold! That "woman" was your wife for nearly thirty years and you say you don't even know her. Typical!

Arnold Now, wait ...

Grace What a fool I was to think you would remember me after our pathetic, brief six months together. (*Breaking down, tearfully*) You bastard, Arnold, you bastard ...

Grace rushes up the stairs in tears and exits

A clap of thunder and we are back in Victorian times. The Lights change, the phone disappears

There is a great wail from the direction of the kitchen from Ilsa, locked in the cellar

Miss Norris (Jess) rushes from the dining-room, distraught

Jess (*as Miss Norris*) Oh, dear God! I cannot bear the sound of this girl's torment a single moment longer! They must release her!

Arnold Quite right!

Jess moves towards the kitchen. As she does so, Dudley (Clem) appears, having followed her from the dining-room. He holds a wine glass

Clem (*as Dudley*) Miss Norris.

Jess (*startled*) Hah!

Clem You rushed from the table, Miss Norris. I trust nothing is wrong?

Jess No, no — I ...

Clem (*offering his arm to Jess*) Allow me to escort you back there, Miss Norris.

Jess (*moving slowly to Clem; to us*) Although every fibre in me was filled with repugnance, I felt myself drawn irresistibly to him like some hapless moth fluttering towards an evil, dark candle.

Clem takes Jess's arm and they head for the dining-room

Clem We are about to drink a toast to the full recovery of my dearest Aunt Elaine. I would hate for you to miss that ...

Clem and Jess go off to the dining-room

Arnold I don't trust him at all. Come to think of it, I don't think I trust any of them.

The front door opens and the Lights change again to the modern setting. The
phone returns

> *Rex (Brevis) enters. With him is another of his nubile assistants, Solo*
> *Pedersen (Vivvi)*

Brevis (*coming into the room; as Rex*) All right, Arnie, how's it going?
Arnold (*seeing Solo*) Oh. Hallo. You're new.

Vivvi nods

Brevis This is Solo, don't for God's sake call her Samantha. Believe it, she's
    affluent in twenty-six languages including six types of regional Chinese.
Arnold Heavens! Useful if you're eating out, then?
Brevis (*to Vivvi*) You want to measure up, Solo?
Vivvi (*as Solo, producing a tape measure*) Sure.
Brevis We ever get a chance to interpolate with these people, Solo's our girl.
Arnold Glad to hear it.
Vivvi (*to Arnold, offering him the tape*) Here.
Arnold What? Oh, yes, I'll hold that for you, yes. Certainly. (*He smiles at*
    her)

Vivvi seems impervious. During the following, Arnold holds the end of the
tape whilst she measures the width and length of the stairs. Brevis,
meanwhile, paces out the hallway as if measuring it

Brevis Hey, Arnie, while we were gone, you see anyone behaving
    contentiously?
Arnold Practically everyone. What are we doing exactly? If you do happen
    to fit stair carpeting on the side, I think we'd be up for that. (*He laughs*)

Vivvi stares at him

Brevis What we're doing, Arnie, is trying to calculate the rough cubic
    capacity area. With these STJ's, understand, they operate within strictly
    limited parabolic parameters. We need to generate ultrasonic waves of up
    to two hundred thousand cycles per second which we then radiate in two
    simulcrumous directions. You follow? We can get even higher base
    affluencies by utilizing a piezoelectric effect and then transmitting it into
    the air via a rudimentary sound box. But that's less effective.
Arnold (*humouring Rex*) Yes, I see. Best to do it that way, then.
Brevis The best, believe me. You want to check upstairs, Solo?
Vivvi Yeah.
Arnold You need any more help with your measuring? No?

Vivvi goes off upstairs without replying

Brevis Twenty-six languages and she won't talk to us in any of them. How about that? Reticulate or what? I'll give the kids a hand out here, won't be long. (*Heading out of the front door, calling*) Come on, guys! Go! Go! Go!

Brevis goes out, leaving the door open

A clap of thunder. The Lights dim briefly to the Victorian state. The phone vanishes

A wail from Ilsa, off, from the kitchen

> *Miss Norris (Jess) rushes, distressed, from the dining-room and up the stairs*

Jess (*as Miss Norris, clasping her hands to her ears*) I cannot bear it! I cannot bear it a single moment longer ...
Arnold Oh, dear!

Jess goes off upstairs

Another clap of thunder. Arnold goes to close the door. As he does so, the Lights return to the daylight state. The candlestick phone reappears

> *DCI Rash (Clem) appears in the doorway*

Arnold, distracted, nearly closes the front door in DCI Rash's face

Arnold Oh, I do beg your pardon. I didn't ...
Clem (*as Jim Rash*) We'll be off shortly, sir. Don't worry.
Arnold Oh, the case all tied up, is it? All solved?
Clem Very nearly. I've asked Miss Green and young Ilsa, now she's returned, to come back in here for a final word, sir.
Arnold Right. I'll leave you to it then, shall I? I just need to check on my ——
Clem No, no. I'd like you to remain here, too, sir.
Arnold Oh? Am I a suspect then?
Clem All will be revealed.

> *Ilsa, in her maid's outfit, enters cautiously from the kitchen*

Ah, come in, girl, come in.

Ilsa (*timidly*) Sir.
Clem It's all right. I'm not going to bite you. Sit down then.

Ilsa hesitates

Arnold (*to Ilsa, quietly*) It's all right, Ilsa, you didn't do it. You're not to
   worry.
Clem Go on, sit down.

Ilsa does so, staring at Arnold

   "Then O, then O, then O my true love said ..."
Ilsa Pardon, sir.
Clem "Till that time come again, She could not live a maid ..." (*Sitting by
   Ilsa*) Tell me, young lady, what made you run away, then?
Ilsa (*tongue-tied*) I — I ...
Clem If someone runs away like that, we might be forgiven for thinking that
   they had a guilty conscience. That they might have done something that
   they're ashamed of. That they were anxious to hide. Is that true, eh?

Ilsa looks again at Arnold

   Why are you looking at him, then? Why are you looking at Mr Hassock?
Ilsa Because I ... (*She hesitates*)
Clem Yes?
Ilsa Because — (*blurting it out*) I think Mr Hassock might have killed
   her ...
Arnold Me?
Clem I see. You think Mr Hassock might have killed his wife, did you?
   Why's that? Why should Mr Hassock want to kill his wife, Ilsa?
Ilsa (*in a tiny voice*) For me.
Clem For you. Why should he kill her for you?
Ilsa Because he loves me.
Clem I see. He told you that, did he?
Ilsa Yes.
Clem And what about you, Ilsa. Do you love him?
Ilsa (*after a slight hesitation*) Yes.
Clem (*standing up and looking at them both*) "Come, love, for now the night
   and day, Play with their pawns of black and white ..."

*DS Fiona Longstaff (Vivvi) and Mavis Green (Grace) enter at the top of
the stairs*

   Ah, Miss Green, thank you so much.

Grace (*as Mavis*) I hope you don't intend to make a habit of this, Chief
   Inspector, summoning us here every ten minutes.
Clem The last time I promise. This time, everyone, do sit down. I insist.

Arnold and Grace do so. Vivvi makes to follow suit

   No, not you, Sergeant, not you. You stand by the front door. Try and stop
   people from running away again.
Vivvi (*as Fiona*) Yes, sir. (*She does so, unhappily*)
Clem Now, I really do apologize for calling you all back again — I know
   you're all very busy people so I won't keep you long. There's just one small
   point concerning that letter from the deceased which you, Miss Green,
   were good enough to read out to us last time ——
Grace Well, what about it?
Clem As I say, one point still eludes me. Silly of me. I'm sure there's an
   explanation. I wonder, would you be kind enough to read it out again?
Grace Again?
Clem I'd be so grateful. If you would. Please. (*He smiles at her*)
Grace Very well. This is a complete waste of all our time, though. Do you
   still have the letter?

Clem		(*Searching his pockets*) Yes, I kept it. I have it some-
		where on me — just a moment ... Ah, here we are.
	(*together*)	There. (*He produces a folded sheet of paper*)
Grace		(*Scrabbling in her handbag*) Oh no, now I don't even
		have them. I had them earlier, I don't know what's
		happened to them ...

Clem What have you lost?
Grace My reading glasses. I can't find them, I must have left them upstairs,
   I'll ——
Clem Oh, no! Don't go to all that trouble. (*Producing a pair of glasses from
   his top pocket*) Here ... Try these. They're my own reading glasses. They
   should do you, they're not that strong ——
Vivvi (*puzzled*) But sir, you don ——
Clem Here, Miss Green! Try these! Please.
Grace (*guardedly*) Very well. Thank you. (*She takes the glasses from Clem
   and, putting them on, opens the sheet of paper and looks at it*) But this isn't
   the letter.
Clem It isn't?
Grace No, it's some — some — it looks like an instruction leaflet for
   something.
Clem Really? I must have given you the wrong — (*Fumbling again in his
   pockets*) Just a second, I'm so sorry ... (*Locating it*) Here we are. This is the
   letter. What on earth can that be, I wonder?
Grace (*offering to return it*) I've no idea. Here ...

Clem (*peering at the paper in her hand*) What can it be? Sorry, I can't without my glasses. Would you mind ...

Grace It's — I don't know what it is ... (*Reading*) "With the lock open, push button in the direction of the arrow brackets A and hold it in this position. Set number wheels to required combination and ——"

Clem (*laughing*) Oh, now! Those are the instructions that came with my new briefcase. How silly can I get ... !

Arnold (*proudly*) I wrote that.

Clem I'm sorry?

Arnold Nothing.

Clem Here we are. I'll take that, Miss Green, I do apologize. Anyway, you're able to read OK with those, that's one thing we've established?

Grace Oh, yes, perfectly fine. They could have been made for me.

Clem Yes, well come to think of it, they probably were.

Grace I beg your pardon.

Clem Made for you. Those are your glasses, Miss Green, which I picked up earlier.

Grace Where from? Did I leave them down here?

Clem No, by the bed. You left them by your sister's bed when you went in there last night with the intention of murdering her, Miss Green.

Silence

Arnold (*incredulously*) Good gracious!

Grace (*tensely*) What on earth are you talking about?

Clem I'm talking about glasses, Miss Green. I'm talking about the deceased's bedroom into which you claimed you never went. But you did go in there, didn't you, sometime during the night? Late on, when your sister was bound to be asleep. What did you do whilst you waited, Miss Green? Sit in your own room for a time, reading perhaps? I suspect you did just that. And then, when the time felt ripe you put down your book and you crept across the landing into her room. There, you took off your reading glasses and you placed those glasses by her bed whilst you attacked her as she slept. Unfortunately, the deceased had left her own glasses by the bed, hadn't she, and you inadvertently placed those glasses, your glasses, next to — (*producing the second, original, pair from his pocket*) — these glasses — her glasses. Later on, having disposed of her, in your haste, instead of picking up those glasses, your own glasses, you picked up these glasses, her glasses. In short, you took the wrong glasses, Miss Green. Too late did you realize your mistake. When you were originally confronted with this letter earlier, you were forced to try to read it with your sister's glasses. But they weren't even reading glasses, alas, but Elaine's everyday glasses. That must have been a nasty moment for you. Was that the first time you realized you'd taken the wrong glasses, was it? So, unable to read anything through these glasses, you were forced to recite the letter from memory. Easier than it sounds because, of course, you originally wrote that letter yourself. That's why I tested you just now by asking you to read something unfamiliar wearing those glasses, purportedly my own glasses, but which you nonetheless had no difficulty in reading. A simple ruse of mine but nevertheless an effective one. Personally, I have no need of glasses, my sergeant was correct for once. Those are your own glasses, admit it, Miss Green. The glasses you left on the deceased's bedside table alongside her own glasses and which you later snatched up, in your panic, in mistake for your glasses. Her glasses. In a word, Miss Green, you have just booked yourself a ringside seat with the public hangman and all for a pair of spectacles.

Grace sits stunned for a moment. Then, suddenly, she leaps from her chair and makes a dash for the front door

Stop her, Sergeant!
Vivvi Oh, no, you don't!

This time, Vivvi overpowers Grace

Ilsa It was her all the time.
Arnold Oh, yes, I guessed that.
Clem Good-afternoon to you both. We'll leave you both in peace now. And — er — just between us — (*he smiles at them*) — I do hope things work out for you two. Be nice to think some good came of all this. Good-bye.
Arnold Good-bye.
Ilsa 'Bye.

Clem moves to the front door and opens it

Clem It's turned into a really pleasant afternoon. Bring her along, Sergeant.
Vivvi (*still holding Grace*) Yes, sir.
Clem (*almost as an afterthought*) Oh — and — well done, Fiona, smart piece of work. "And all the charms of face or voice, Which I in others see, Are but the recollected choice, Of what I felt for thee ..."

Clem goes out

Vivvi (*weeping with happiness*) Isn't he wonderful? (*To Grace*) Come on, you!

Vivvi and Grace go out

Ilsa and Arnold are now standing alone. Ilsa turns to Arnold who looks at her rather apprehensively

Ilsa (*her face glowing with happiness*) Oh, sir! (*Moving to him a little*) Oh, sir! Sir!

Arnold Yes. Well, Ilsa, I think you should be getting on with ... shouldn't you?

Ilsa Yes, sir. (*She moves happily to the kitchen doorway, then turns back to him, radiantly*) Oh, sir!

She hurries out

Arnold Oh, dear.

Thunder. The Lights change again to the Victorian candle-lit setting. The phone disappears

Jess (Miss Norris) enters from the dining-room

Jess (*as Miss Norris, to us*) I had wearied of my tapestry work that evening and was making my way to bed when I chanced upon a significant meeting between the saintly Mr Arnold and his dear friend, Dr Thomas Goodpiece ... I drew back into the shadows to listen. (*She draws back into the shadows*)

Dr Goodpiece (Brevis) enters down the stairs

Brevis (*as Goodpiece*) Arnold, my good friend ...

Arnold Oh, it's you again ...

Brevis I have been tending to your sister. She is safely on the road to recovery.

Arnold Good, I'm very happy for her.

Brevis Arnold, there is a matter I wish to discuss with you, one of extreme gravity ...

Arnold Oh, yes?

Brevis I now suspect that the girl Ilsa is innocent ...

Arnold Well, I could have told you that all along.

Brevis Wait! There is a plot afoot, Arnold, a devilish plot not only to discredit and incriminate her but further to drive the girl from her mind.

From the direction of the kitchen comes a wail from Ilsa

Hark at her, poor creature! What should we do for the best?

Arnold I think it would be a good idea to let her out of the cellar for a start.

Brevis Indeed. I will summon Mrs Dimchurch immediately. (*He moves to the kitchen doorway and calls*)

*During Jess's following speech, in dumbshow Mrs Dimchurch (Vivvi)
enters and Brevis sends her off, relieved, to release Ilsa*

Jess (*to us*) I watched as Dr Goodpiece summoned Mrs Dimchurch and
ordered her to release the poor tormented creature from her prison. Mrs
Dimchurch, not normally the most demonstrative of women, betrayed on
this occasion an expression of extreme relief, possibly in part the result of
having listened to the child screaming continuously for several hours.

Brevis Arnold, I have a scheme which, if you are agreeable, I will put into
effect.

Arnold What's that?

Brevis We know, from the girl's own admission, that these voices — these
apparitions, these unexplained visitations — only occur when she is alone.
They are never witnessed by another living soul.

Arnold True.

Brevis I propose, therefore, to lay a trap. We will leave her here by herself,
apparently alone. Meanwhile we shall lie in wait, you and I, to see what
transpires. Maybe for once, my friend, we can ourselves be witness to these
mysterious happenings.

Arnold Oh, I see. That's a good idea. You think Ilsa will be up for that?

Brevis Leave the child to me. I will reassure her. Hush, now, she comes!

Vivvi returns leading Ilsa, who looks a bit the worse for wear

Brevis speaks to Ilsa in dumbshow under the next, gradually persuading her

Vivvi leaves

Jess (*to us*) My eyes welled with tears at the sight of this once lively girl who
now, tortured, tormented and cruelly imprisoned as she had been, appeared
so broken in spirit. How I longed, at that moment, to rush forward and clasp
her to my own bosom, but caution ruled my heart. It was with relief that I
saw the doctor speak gently and kindly to the girl. Softly persuading her to
acquiesce to his scheme, whilst forswearing upon the very lives of both him
and kindly Mr Arnold that no harm would possibly befall her.

Brevis You will do it, Ilsa? For us?

Ilsa (*very faintly*) Very well ...

Brevis (*drawing Ilsa to a chair in the middle of the hall*) Thank you. Please,
be seated here.

Ilsa sits

We will not be far away, child, I swear it. Come, Arnold, let us conceal
ourselves and wait.

Arnold We'll just be round here, Ilsa. (*Indicating*) Round here.

Brevis and Arnold draw back into the shadows by the kitchen doorway. Ilsa is left alone in the middle of the hall

Jess (*to us*) Minutes passed, turning to what seemed like hours. If I had not heard the dining-room clock strike first the quarter, the half and then the three quarter hour in turn, I would have sworn that dawn was about to break. The child's head slumped once or twice and I feared she might have fallen asleep through sheer exhaustion. What then would have become of Dr Goodpiece's scheme? Then, just as it seemed that all our patience, our discomfort was in vain, I noticed Ilsa sit up slightly in her chair, listening intently, as if she alone had heard or seen something, something which had eluded the rest of us. Could it really be true that these mysterious events were in fact the result of her own fevered imaginings? Then, quite suddenly ——

Thunder. The front door slams open. The wind howls

Standing in the doorway is a tall Figure in a long cloak, the hood pulled up to cover its head and face. The Figure steps in through the doorway and faces Ilsa

Ilsa moans slightly

The Figure (*in a sepulchral whisper*) Ilsa ... Ilsa ...
Ilsa What do you want? What do you want of me?
The Figure (*extending its hand to her*) Ilsa ...
Arnold Heavens!
Brevis Sssshhh!
Jess (*to us*) I confess, I all but cried out but found myself instead transfixed like the others upon the ghastly figure which now threatened Ilsa.
Ilsa Tell me what you want. Why are you here?
The Figure I am here to take you, Ilsa. Back to whence you came — whence you belong. To the very gutter, the sewer from which you first crawled ...
Ilsa (*drawing back*) No ... no ...
The Figure You cannot deny me, Ilsa. Behold, I bring you a gift.

The Figure throws its hood back revealing its face for the first time. It has a long mane of hair and is heavily bearded and bushy-browed

Ilsa No ...
The Figure Heeeerrre ...

The Figure lifts both hands to its face and then quite slowly and deliberately removes its head and, holding out its arms, offers it to Ilsa. Ilsa screams. So do Jess and Arnold. Brevis springs from the shadows and confronts The Figure

Brevis (*urgently*) Quickly, my friend! We have him, now! We have the devil!

Arnold moves forward rather reluctantly to assist. Brevis takes the head from The Figure's hands

Aha! Just as I thought, you fiend!

Brevis hands the head to Arnold who reacts. Ilsa rises and draws back; Jess steps forward to hold and comfort her. Brevis tackles The Figure itself

(*As they struggle*) Oh no, my friend, not this time. No longer will you seek to terrify the weak and vulnerable. Never — (*struggling triumphantly*) — again!

Dudley (Clem) is unmasked

(*Amazed*) Dudley!

Jess ⎫ (*incredulous*) Dudley!
Ilsa ⎭

Arnold Oh, I knew it was Dudley ...

Brevis You vile, fiendish, hell-like creature.

Arnold ... it couldn't have been anyone else but Dudley.

Brevis Witness what you have done to this innocent girl! What diabolical plot have you engendered ...?

Clem (*as Dudley*) Oh, a simple one, my dear doctor, merely to drive her to madness. She stood to inherit, you see, what was rightfully mine. I watched her as she wormed and squirmed her way into all your hearts, with her simpering manner and her soft talk, seeping like poison into the hearts of my gullible Aunt Elaine and that pliable, susceptible fool of an uncle. And why? Why should they turn their favours to her? Because I am not beautiful? I am not soft spoken as she? Unpractised in the use of weasel flattery or squirrel smiles? I curse her, she born in the gutter, who has inherited everything. Whereas I, so deformed of spirit ... I curse her! (*To Jess*) And you, madam! (*To Brevis*) And you, sir! (*To Arnold*) And you, Uncle! My curse upon you all! My life is wasted! I have wasted my life, do you hear? Wasted! Wasted!

Clem sweeps out, slamming the front door behind him. A final clap of thunder

Arnold Good riddance.

Brevis Wisely spoken, my friend. (*Approaching Ilsa and Jess*) Well, young mistress, I suspect your nightmare is now passed. One thing is certain, we will surely not see your cousin again in these parts. At least, not so long as your uncle and I shall live.

Ilsa Thank you, Doctor.

Brevis My pleasure, Miss Ilsa. I declare, Miss Norris, your pupil is in need of rest after her ordeal. Be so good as to escort her to her room.

Jess Of course, Doctor.

Jess heads towards the stairs, leading Ilsa, during the following

Brevis moves to Arnold and takes from him the Figure's head which he is still holding

Brevis Here, my friend. Let me relieve you of that.

Arnold Thank you.

Brevis (*moving to the front door, examining the head*) Hmmm! Papier mâché, I do believe. Simple but effective. Excuse me, ladies. I will ensure that our unwanted guest has quit the premises for ever. Good-night to you both. (*Opening the front door and stepping out*) Ah! I do believe this wretched storm is clearing at last ...

Brevis exits, closing the door behind him

Arnold What a nice man ...

Ilsa (*turning on the stairs*) Uncle ——

Arnold — er — (*Realizing to whom she is referring*) Oh, yes?

Ilsa (*trying to speak*) I — I ... Oh, Uncle!

Ilsa rushes back down the stairs and hugs the rather startled Arnold

Dear, dear, dear sweet uncle. Thank you. (*Impetuously she kisses him on the cheek*)

Arnold Oh, yes. Better get off to bed now, Ilsa. Good-night.

Ilsa (*her eyes filled with tears*) Good-night, Uncle. (*She rushes back to Jess*)

Jess Good-night, sir. (*To us*) And so, dear reader, we left the uncle a smiling, contented man, secure in the knowledge that his house was finally purged forever of hatred, to be filled once again with Christian love.

Ilsa and Jess go off upstairs

The Lights change back to their modern state. The phone returns

Arnold (*touched*) Ah! Well, that's that then. I think I'll ...

The front door opens and Rhona Reed (Grace) and Solo Pedersen (Vivvi) enter. They carry two pieces of technical equipment each, detectors on stands (STJ's), plus three separate coils of cable

Grace (*as Rhona*) Hi, baby!

Vivvi nods

Arnold Oh, no, it's you lot. I'd forgotten about you.

Grace (*to Vivvi*) Two at the bottom of the stairs and two in the bedroom doorway.

Vivvi (*as Solo*) Sure.

Grace I'll set these up here. Here, Solo — (*tossing Grace a coil of cable*) — use a separate power source for those. Run it out the window.

Vivvi Sure.

Vivvi goes off upstairs with the two detectors and the coil of cable over her shoulder

Arnold watches this anxiously

Arnold I hope you're not going to make too much mess ...

Grace sets her two stands at the bottom of the stairs, connects the cables to them and starts to run these back to the front door during the following

Grace (*as she sets up*) It's all in hand, Arnie. These are basic STJ detectors. They're tuned to pick up any type of alien activity. We'll be putting just the six in this house, two there, two by the door here and two upstairs ... The rest we're deploying outside ...

At this point, Sandy Triffin (Zap) (Clem) enters. He is dressed like the others. He carries two more stands with wires trailing from them

Clem (*as Zap, to Grace*) Here. You want these.

Grace Sure. (*Indicating*) Put them there, Zap.

Arnold How many more of you are there?

Clem (*putting down the stands*) Hi!

Grace Arnie, this is Zap. Zap, also known as Sandy, take your pick. Zap — Arnie. Arnie — Sandy.

Clem Hi!

Arnold Hi!

Grace Here. Connect these, will you?

Grace hands Clem the two cables connected to the stands she has set by the stairs

Clem (*taking them*) Sure. (*To Arnold*) Good to meet you, Arnie. Stay cool.
Arnold I will if you keep leaving that door open.

Clem goes off taking the cables

Vivvi enters and comes back down the stairs

Grace (*to Vivvi*) All set there?
Vivvi Sure.
Arnold What happens now?
Grace We pray for something to happen — (*to Vivvi*) — fetch the gizmo,
Solo.
Vivvi Sure.

Vivvi goes out again

Grace If something predisposes itself between either of these pairs of
sensors — then these lights will flash ...
Arnold They haven't flashed yet.
Grace What?
Arnold She just walked between them and nothing happened.
Grace I hope not. She's human. More or less. They're set for alien
metabolism. Silicone-based, you see?
Arnold Oh. I see.

Vivvi returns with a hand-held gadget

Vivvi (*stopping in the doorway*) OK?
Grace Sure. Give it a try.

*Vivvi waves the gadget between the door sensors. The lights on the sensors
flash*

Arnold Ah!
Grace Silicone, you see.

Vivvi does the same at the foot of the stairs. Those bulbs flash in turn

That's a silicone-based conceptor. OK. Check upstairs, Solo.
Vivvi Sure.

Vivvi goes back upstairs and exits

Clem comes through the front door

Clem Ready to roll!

Grace The outside sensors working?

Clem All two hundred. I ran them from here to the village. Nothing gets in or out of the area without our cognizing. I'll be in the van, start monitoring.

Grace K.I.T.

Clem (*heading back out*) S.U.R.

Rex (Brevis) enters, passing Clem

Hi, chief.

Clem exits

Brevis (*as Rex*) OK, Zap?

Clem (*off*) OK.

Brevis Arnie, how you doing?

Arnold Very well, thank you. Just been seeing your equipment in action. Very impressive.

Brevis You're impressed?

Arnold Oh, yes.

Brevis Let's hope these things are impressed, that's all.

Vivvi returns at the top of the stairs

(*To her*) Solo, stay up there.

Vivvi Sure.

Brevis I want all these exits fortificated and sealed. Rhona, you take the front door. Remain outside the sensorial areas. Arnie, you want to take that doorway? (*He points to the kitchen doorway*)

Arnold Oh, right. (*He moves as directed*)

Brevis I'll take this one. (*He moves to the dining-room doorway*) Rhona, hit the lights.

Grace Chief.

Grace operates the light switch inside the front door. The room goes into virtual darkness. Arnold is in the kitchen doorway, Brevis in the dining-room doorway, Grace at the front door and Vivvi at the top of the stairs

Good. This way, nothing gets in or out. Especially out. If it's still in here, it stays in.

Arnold How long are we likely to be?

Brevis Who knows? Maybe all night.

Arnold Oh no ...

Brevis What's the matter, Arnie? You want your mother back, don't you?

Arnold Oh, yes. I'm just not totally convinced she's actually gone ...

Grace She's gone, baby. Believe me, she's gone. God knows what
those ——

Suddenly, the sensors at the bottom of the stairs flash on and off briefly

Brevis Hey! What was *that?*
Grace You doing anything up there, Solo?
Vivvi No.
Brevis (*tense*) Something's here, then. Something's in here. With us.

Silence. They wait and listen

See anything, Arnie?
Arnold No, I can't even see my feet. Why don't we put the lights on?
Brevis No! Don't touch the lights! Touch the lights we're all dead. Rhona?
Grace I can — I think I can hear something breathing ... I'm not sure, it might
be ——

The sensor lights by the front door flash

(*Crying out, as if hit*) Ah! It's out the front door. It's out the front door.
Brevis Don't let it get away ! Solo! It's invisible! The bastard made itself
invisible! Go! Go! Go!

*Grace rushes out of the front door followed by Brevis and Vivvi, all
shouting "Go, go, go!"*

Arnold is left alone in the dark

Arnold (*rather nervously*) Hallo! Is anyone there? Hallo. Oh, I can't stand
here in the dark all night. I'm going to risk it.

Arnold switches on the lights again at a switch by the kitchen doorway

Brevis enters, breathless

Brevis They got it. Caught it. Couldn't profligate its invisibility for more than
a few yards. Ran straight into Zap. He brought it down. Disabled it.
Arnold I hope it's all right.
Brevis They're putting it into a containment pod. Then they'll bring it in here,
take a look at it. (*Looking up*) More important — I wonder if *they* know
what's happened yet.
Arnold Who's they?

Brevis Five hundred miles out. Up there in the mother ship. I wonder if they've already realized. I assume they have, they don't miss much.

Arnold What'll they do then? Destroy the entire world? That's what they usually do, isn't it?

Brevis My proficient hope is they'll do a trade. That captured thing out there for your mother, Arnie. That's my hope. I guess that's your hope too, huh?

Arnold How will we know? If they want to trade?

Brevis Your mother will come walking through that door. That's how we'll know, Arnie.

Grace, Vivvi and Clem enter. They are pushing a large spherical "containment pod", not dissimilar to a large walnut. A thick connecting cable trails behind it

Grace (*as they wheel it in*) All right. Bit further. In the middle here. That's it! That'll do.

They come to rest. The pod pulses slightly with internal light. Vivvi immediately starts to disconnect the sensors from the stairs

Right, Solo, let's get these stowed.

Grace disconnects the sensors in the doorway

Vivvi and Grace go out, coiling their respective cables

Brevis Will it be all right in there?

Clem Sealed tight.

Arnold I hope it can breathe. It's a bit snug, isn't it? Not much air.

Clem We're feeding in methane life support, through the umblicical there. It's not going to suffocate. Rex, are we seriously going to trade it back? I mean, the research we could do on this thing ...

Brevis (*solemnly*) There's a human life at stake here, Zap. Nothing's more important than a human life.

Clem (*chastened*) Right. Once we abandon that sacred principle then we're behaving no better than the rest of the universe. You're right, of course.

Grace and Vivvi return

Grace We locked the vehicle.

Arnold It'll be safe enough out there.

Brevis You never can tell. Sometimes there's kids.

Grace They let down the tyres.

Vivvi Bastards.
Brevis Come on, Solo, lighten up. They're kids, just kids ...
Clem You think they know? Up there? That we have it?
Brevis They do by now.

Vivvi, Clem and Arnold sit. Grace loiters by the door. Brevis sits at the piano

(*Opening the lid*) Hey. Nice piano, Arnie.
Arnold My mother's.
Brevis Nice. Let's hope they left her with fingers.
Grace You going to play us something, Rex?
Brevis I don't think so.
Grace Go on. While we're waiting. (*To Arnold*) He's good. Sometimes when we're all a little low, you know, in the Slough of Despond, he ... Go ahead, Rex.
Clem Go on.
Brevis Well ...

Brevis is about to play when there is a banging on the front door

(*Rising, excitedly*) It's her! That has to be her! Let her in, Rhona!

Grace opens the door

Elaine (Jess) is standing there in her night-dress, grubby and dazed. She staggers in

Jess (*as Elaine, hoarsely*) Help me, please!
Grace It's her!
Clem It's her!
Brevis Praise be! It's her!
Arnold Who is it?
Brevis It's your mother, Arnie. It's your mother!
Arnold That's not my mother!
Grace It's your mother, baby!
Arnold She's nothing like my mother.
Brevis Dear God, what are they doing to us? A man can't even recognize his own mother! OK. Rhona, help her upstairs. The old lady needs rest. I'll check her over, don't worry, Arnold. But first things first. They kept their side of the bargain, we need to keep ours.

Grace helps Jess up the stairs

Jess goes off

Grace stops to watch the following

Vivvi We do?
Brevis Yes, we do, Solo, we do. Zap, open the chamber. Let the thing out.
   At least we can take a look at it, before we let it go.
Clem You're sure?
Brevis Sure as I've ever been.
Clem Right. Here we go. Stand back.

Clem slowly opens the lid of the case which swings in under itself. The pod is now hemispherical and resembles a half walnut

(*Stepping back, in horror*) Oh, dear heaven! What is it in there?

A strange figure (Ilsa) sits up in the shell. She has a green suit and a red pointed hat

Ilsa (*in a funny little voice*) Hatcha noot screeee! (*Literally: Wish me luck*)

A pause

Grace (*overjoyed*) It's Doblin the Goblin!
All Doblin the Goblin!

Brevis sits down at the piano again. He begins to play and sing the intro. to his song again. Everyone joins in, including Ilsa and Arnold. Grace comes down the stairs

The song soon runs out of lyrics as before but no-one seems concerned and just carries on singing la-la-la

All (*singing*)   There'll be light at the end of the tunnel.
                      Yes, it's bright, have no fear every one'll
                      Reach the end, my dear friend,
                      As we turn that final bend,
                      There'll be light! Precious light! There'll be light!
                      La-la-la-la-la-la-la — Cheerio!
                      La-la-la-la-la-la-la — Here I go!
                      La-la-la-la-la-la-la — *etc. etc.*

Brevis leaves the piano at some stage but the music, which has now been augmented, continues

Indeed, it all turns into something quite choreographic as Ilsa produces a paddle from her coracle and starts to steer Doblin's craft out through the front door. Vivvi, Grace, Clem and Brevis pick up the sensors and up-end them. The feet on each of these fall away to become flower petals, reminiscent of large buttercups. Jess enters and comes downstairs, dressed as a squirrel

Ilsa paddles out of sight

The others remain in the front doorway, waving and smiling. Only Arnold holds back slightly, staying in the centre of the room

At the end of the song, the five remaining turn and wave good-bye to Arnold as well and then exit, closing the front door

Silence

Arnold is left alone

Arnold Oh, well. Nice to finish with a sing song.

In a second, he goes to the front door and opens it again to check if there's anyone out there

There is the sound of a motorbike arriving

(*Calling*) Oh, hallo, Kev! Yes. She's just getting her coat. (*He moves to the kitchen doorway. Calling*) Ilsa! He's here!

Ilsa comes in from the kitchen, pulling on her coat

Ilsa Just coming. (*She finishes buttoning her coat*) Good. Right. I'll be off then. Nothing else was there?
Arnold No, nothing else, thank you, Ilsa.
Ilsa Well. Happy Christmas then, Arnold, eh? (*She smiles at him*)
Arnold (*smiling at her*) Yes, a happy Christmas to you too, Ilsa.

Awkwardly and rather impetuously, Ilsa kisses Arnold's cheek and then, as if embarrassed by this display of affection, she hurries out through the door

Ilsa (*as she goes*) 'Night!
Arnold 'Night! (*Softly*) Happy Christmas. (*He watches her through the door*)

The motorbike revs and departs

Arnold waves and then finally closes the door. He moves back to the middle of the room and is about to straighten the furniture when there is thumping on the floor of the room above

(*Moving to the stairs, calling*) All right, Mother. Just coming. They've all gone now. Just coming ... (*Climbing the stairs*) No, no ... quite a quiet meeting, really. Nothing unusual ...

Arnold goes off

Black-out

FURNITURE AND PROPERTY LIST

ACT I

On stage: Armchairs
Upright chairs
Sideboard. *On it*: modern phone
Occasional tables
Small grand piano
Coathooks
Uninteresting pictures

Off stage: Motorbike helmet, carrier bag containing very small artificial Christmas tree with battery lights in a plastic pot (**Ilsa**)
Chair (**Ilsa**)
Briefcase containing notes, paper bag containing eggs (**Jess**)
Artist's cardboard portfolio containing brightly-coloured illustrations (**Grace**)
Briefcase containing freshly-typed sheets of text and stapled synopses (**Clem**)
Large shoulder bag containing notebook and pencil (**Vivvi**)
Tray with six cups, coffee pot, milk, sugar, six side plates, pre-heated shop-made mince pies (**Ilsa**)
Single candlestick with candle, large old-fashioned kitchen knife (**Ilsa**)

Personal: **Arnold**: watch (worn throughout)

ACT II

Strike: Phone

Off stage: Wine glass (**Clem**)
Four detectors on stands with flower-petal feet, three coils of cable (**Vivvi** and **Grace**)
Two detectors with flower-petal feet, with wires (**Clem**)
Hand-held gadget (**Vivvi**)
Containment pod containing paddle (**Grace**, **Vivvi** and **Clem**)

Personal: **Grace**: handbag containing glasses
Clem: letter, folded sheet of paper, two pairs of glasses; papier mâché head
Vivvi: tape measure

During lighting change p. 43

Set: Old-fashioned candlestick phone

During lighting change p. 48

Strike: Candlestick phone

Set: Modern phone

During lighting change p. 49

Strike: Modern phone

During lighting change p. 50

Set: Modern phone

During lighting change p. 51

Strike: Modern candlestick phone

During lighting change p. 52

Set: Candlestick phone

During lighting change p. 55

Strike: Candlestick phone

During lighting change p. 56

Set: Modern phone

During lighting change p. 57

Strike: Modern phone

During second lighting change p. 57

Set: Candlestick phone

During lighting change p. 62

Strike: Candlestick phone

During lighting change p. 66

Set: Modern phone

LIGHTING PLOT

Practical fittings required: flashing lights on sensors, interior lights on containment pod
One interior with exterior window backing. The same throughout

ACT I

To open: General interior lighting; darkness on window backing

Cue 1	Loud clap of thunder *Black-out*	(Page 36)
Cue 2	**Arnold**: "If I can see the way." *Bring up candle glow effect behind kitchen door*	(Page 36)
Cue 3	**Ilsa** enters with candle *Bring up covering spot on candle*	(Page 36)
Cue 4	**Brevis** appears with candelabra *Bring up covering spot on candelabra*	(Page 36)
Cue 5	**Arnold**: "Good gracious!" *Black-out*	(Page 37)

ACT II

To open: Darkness

Cue 6	**Arnold**: "Good gracious." *Bring up candlelight effect and spot on **Jess***	(Page 38)
Cue 7	Thunder *Change lights to daylight (1930s) effect with sun streaming through windows; daylight effect on window backing*	(Page 43)
Cue 8	**Clem** and **Vivvi** exit *Dip lights and re-establish with night-time effect similar to – but not quite the same as — the Act I setting*	(Page 47)
Cue 9	Thunder *Lights return to Victorian setting; spot on **Jess***	(Page 49)

Cue 10	**Arnold**: "We haven't got a cellar." *Lights change to modern setting*	(Page 50)
Cue 11	**Arnold** moves to the stairs *Lights change to Victorian setting*	(Page 51)
Cue 12	**Miss Norris** appears in dining-room doorway *Bring up light on* **Miss Norris**	(Page 51)
Cue 13	**Arnold** moves towards the kitchen *Lights change to daylight (1930s) setting*	(Page 52)
Cue 14	Thunder *Lights change to Victorian setting*	(Page 55)
Cue 15	Front door opens *Lights change to modern setting*	(Page 56)
Cue 16	Clap of thunder *Lights dim to Victorian state*	(Page 57)
Cue 17	Clap of thunder *Lights dim to daylight (1930s) setting*	(Page 57)
Cue 18	Thunder *Lights dim to Victorian state*	(Page 62)
Cue 19	**Ilsa** and **Jess** go off upstairs *Lights return to their modern setting*	(Page 66)
Cue 20	**Vivvi** waves the gadget between the door sensors *Lights flash on sensors*	(Page 68)
Cue 21	**Vivvi** waves the gadget between the sensors on the stairs *Lights flash on sensors*	(Page 68)
Cue 22	**Grace** operates the light switch *Virtual darkness*	(Page 69)
Cue 23	**Grace**: "God knows what those ——" *Sensors at the bottom of the stairs flash*	(Page 70)
Cue 24	**Grace**: " … I'm not sure, it might be …" *Sensors by the front door flash*	(Page 70)
Cue 25	**Arnold** switches the lights on *Bring up interior lights*	(Page 70)

Cue 26   Pod comes to rest   (Page 71)
              Pulsing light inside pod

Cue 27   **Arnold** exits   (Page 75)
              Black-out

EFFECTS PLOT

ACT I

Cue 1   **Arnold**: " … Arnold … one, two …"   (Page 2)
Doorbell

Cue 2   **Ilsa**: "Give her my love!"   (Page 2)
Motorbike roaring off

Cue 3   **Ilsa** goes off to the dining-room   (Page 3)
Thumping from the floor above

Cue 4   **Ilsa**:"Right."   (Page 6)
More thumping from the floor above

Cue 5   **Ilsa** and **Arnold** smile at each other   (Page 6)
Thumping from the floor above

Cue 5   **Arnold**: "We're hardly ——"   (Page 7)
Doorbell

Cue 6   **Jess**: " … you have to love her."   (Page 8)
Doorbell

Cue 7   **Grace** sits   (Page 9)
Doorbell

Cue 8   **Arnold**: "Too cold to stand out there."   (Page 10)
Doorbell

Cue 9   **Jess**: "All I'm saying is ——"   (Page 15)
Doorbell

Cue 10   **Arnold**: "If we could ——"   (Page 22)
Sudden thumping from the floor above

Cue 11   **Arnold**: "She really doesn't need to wash up …"   (Page 35)
Rumble of thunder

Cue 12   **Arnold** returns from the dining-room   (Page 35)
Louder thunder

Cue 13   **Arnold** exits   (Page 35)
            Much louder clap of thunder

Cue 14   Black-out   (Page 36)
            Crash from dining-room

ACT II

Cue 15   **Jess** goes out to the dining-room   (Page 43)
            Thunder

Cue 16   **Arnold**: "What ——?"   (Page 43)
            Doorbell — a different ring from before

Cue 17   **Arnold**: "What's that, then?"   (Page 43)
            Doorbell rings again

Cue 18   **Arnold**: "Back to normal, thank goodness!"   (Page 48)
            "Normal" doorbell rings

Cue 19   **Arnold**: "I'm being assaulted now."   (Page 49)
            Thunder

Cue 21   **Arnold** moves to the stairs   (Page 51)
            Thunder

Cue 22   **Grace** rushes up the stairs and exits   (Page 55)
            Thunder

Cue 23   **Brevis** goes out   (Page 57)
            Clap of thunder

Cue 24   **Arnold**: "Oh, dear."   (Page 62)
            Thunder

Cue 25   **Jess**: "Then, quite suddenly ——"   (Page 64)
            Thunder. Wind howls

Cue 26   **Clem** sweeps out and slams the door   (Page 65)
            Clap of thunder

Cue 27   During song   (Page 73)
            Bring up recorded music to augment the piano

Cue 28   **Arnold** looks out of the front door   (Page 74)
            Sound of motorbike arriving

Cue 29   **Arnold** watches **Ilsa** through the door   (Page 75)
Motorbike revs and departs

Cue 30   **Arnold** makes to straighten the furniture   (Page 75)
Thumping from the floor above